EXCELLENT PREACHING

*PROCLAIMING THE GOSPEL
IN ITS CONTEXT & OURS*

CRAIG G. BARTHOLOMEW

Excellent Preaching: Proclaiming the Gospel in Its Context and Ours

Copyright 2015 Craig G. Bartholomew

Lexham Press, 1313 Commercial St., Bellingham, WA 98225
LexhamPress.com

Print ISBN 978-1-57-799650-7
Digital ISBN 978-1-57-799651-4

Lexham Editorial Team: Abigail Stocker
Cover Design: Micah Ellis
Typesetting: ProjectLuz.com

CONTENTS

Foreword v

Preface vii

Introduction 1

The Destination, the Plane, and the Cargo 6

The Captain 13

The View from Arrivals 17

The Airport: Contextualization 37

Landing the Plane: Some Examples 54

Conclusion 66

Appendix A: Suggested Reading 69

Appendix B: An Expanded Apostles' Creed 70

Endnotes 72

About the Author 77

To the congregation of St. Georges, Burlington, of which it is a privilege to be a part.

FOREWORD

Becoming biblically grounded is a top priority for the churches and people in our diocese, the Anglican Network in Canada (ANiC). Archbishop Thomas Cranmer's prayer that God would cause us to "read, mark, learn, and inwardly digest" the Scriptures marks the Anglican reformation now under way.

We are seeking to take seriously the exhortation of the Apostle Paul to his young protégé Timothy: "Do your best to present yourself to God as one approved, a worker who has no need to be ashamed, rightly handling the word of truth" (2 Tim 2:15 ESV). Later in the same epistle Paul says: "All Scripture is God-breathed and is useful for teaching, rebuking, correcting and training in righteousness, so that the servant of God may be thoroughly equipped for every good work" (2 Tim 3:16–17).

I am so grateful that one of our ANiC clergy is the Rev. Dr. Craig Bartholomew. Craig is the author of many important books and an esteemed professor of philosophy, theology, and religion at Redeemer University College. His passion is to wisely and faithfully interpret and apply the Word of God under the leading of the Holy Spirit. This is seen consistently in all his teaching and writing.

The metaphor of "landing the plane" is a very helpful one. Clearly it has to do with taking the Word we have heard and applying it wisely and faithfully. As one who does far more flying than I like, I would not like to remain in a circling plane, never landing at the destination. As a preacher, I must admit that far too often I've left the plane circling.

This book is a strong challenge—to me and others—to make sure the plane lands at the right destination.

When I invited Craig Bartholomew to address this topic at our 2015 Diocesan Synod, I was fully expecting excellent presentations. I had never anticipated that it would be possible for these important presentations to be published in the form of a book. I am very grateful to Professor Bartholomew and to Lexham Press for producing this wonderful book, which will multiply the benefit of this teaching far and wide. I am delighted! And I highly commend *Excellent Preaching: Proclaiming the Gospel in Its Context and Ours*.

I trust that this book will be read and pondered and will inform our approach to applying the Bible. For then we will be truly disciples of Jesus—and truly free. For he said: "If you hold to my teaching, you are really my disciples. Then you will know the truth, and the truth will set you free" (John 8:31–32).

The Right Rev. Charlie Masters
Diocesan Bishop
Anglican Network in Canada

PREFACE

This book has its origins in a gracious invitation by Bishop Charlie Masters to present the keynote lectures at the 2015 Synod of the Anglican Network in Canada in Vancouver. In discussion with John Barry of Lexham Press the idea emerged of producing a small book on the topic. I am grateful to Bishop Charlie and to John for their roles in stimulating me to produce this work. Gillian Fernie was also wonderfully helpful in closely reading and helping to make this book more accessible. I am indebted to a conversation several years ago with Christopher Wright for helping shape the book as well.

Readers should note that I discuss preaching in far more theoretical detail in the final chapter of my *Introducing Biblical Hermeneutics* (Grand Rapids: Baker Academic, 2015), which will be published at about the same time as this book. For detailed references to current debates and resources about preaching, readers should consult that chapter.

I can think of few things more important than a renaissance of preaching in our day. My hope is that this small work will contribute in some measure in that direction. Moses and Jesus would remind us that we do not live simply by bread alone but by every word that proceeds from the mouth of God. Some perceptive analysts argue that for the first time in history we in the West are trying to live and form societies "by bread alone." In such a context we should not expect preaching to be a priority—but in truth, this increases the need for really good preaching.

In this book, I aim to raise the bar high and to evoke for preachers their holy and high calling. Good preaching is exceptionally hard work and calls for the best we can offer in our service of God. It would be wonderful if this small work would stimulate us to think hard, work hard, and pray hard together as we preach and listen to God's Word.

Craig G. Bartholomew
KwaZulu Natal, South Africa
July 2015

INTRODUCTION

Proverbs 30:1–6, a much-neglected but remarkable passage, evokes our need for God's Word:

> The sayings of Agur son of Jakeh—an inspired
> utterance.
> This man's utterance to Ithiel:
> "I am weary, God,
>   but I can prevail.
> Surely I am only a brute, not a man;
>   I do not have human understanding.
> I have not learned wisdom,
>   nor have I attained to the knowledge of the Holy
>   One.
> Who has gone up to heaven and come down?
>   Whose hands have gathered up the wind?
> Who has wrapped up the waters in a cloak?
>   Who has established all the ends of the earth?
> What is his name, and what is the name of his son?
>   Surely you know!
>
> "Every word of God is flawless;
>   he is a shield to those who take refuge in him.
> Do not add to his words,
>   or he will rebuke you and prove you a liar."

In this rich passage, which rewards careful reflection, Agur reveals a profound understanding of his limits as a human being and the weariness that results (Prov 30:1) from trying to live without God's Word. No matter how bright and enlightened we may be, we have not gone up to heaven and come down again; we have not gathered up the wind and wrapped up the waters in a cloak; we have not established the ends of the earth. In Ecclesiastes, a common metaphor that the Teacher uses for his autonomous, wearying search for wisdom is that it is like "a chasing after the wind" (see, for example, Eccl 2:26). *Human* understanding and wisdom require input from outside the creation, from the Holy One (Prov 30:3), because they are created, and humans are not the Creator (Prov 30:4). This means that God's Word—which, in the Hebrew, literally means "refined" and, thus, pure and without any flaw (Prov 30:5)—is of inestimable value for human life and understanding in all their dimensions.

It is hard to express today the importance of the Bible as the Word of God for both the church and the world. Amid a global resurgence of religion—not least Christianity—the tired West continues to lumber along the path of vacuous secularism, as evidenced by, for example, New Atheism. In the depths of our individualism and global consumer culture, it is a challenge of the imagination to see the great need for and relevance of the Word of God. To a significant extent modernity is built on a desire to marginalize and obliterate God from the public dimensions of life, and to a large extent—although not without cost—it has succeeded.[1]

In the vital circles of missiology (the study of mission), serious critique of Western culture really only took hold after the International Missionary Council in Tambaram in 1938. Two world wars and the Holocaust now make it impossible to assume that Western culture is superior, basically Christian, or even neutral. The disasters and tragedies that beset the West in the 20th century—making it, in some estimates, the most brutal in history—affected the Western church in at least two major ways. Walter E. Williams, for example, noted in 2000 that "the 20th century … will be remembered for unprecedented technical progress, advance of knowledge and improvements in the living standards. It will also be remembered as mankind's most brutal century. International and civil wars have yielded a death toll of roughly 50 million lives. As tragic as that number is, it's small in comparison to the number of people murdered by their own government."[2] On the one hand, the close association of Christianity with the West meant that as Western culture was evaluated and criticized, so was Christianity. The question of the uniqueness of Jesus is at the heart of Christian belief—hence the demise within many mainline denominations of a firm commitment to the "question of the uniqueness, sufficiency and finality of Jesus Christ as the Lord and Saviour of the world."[3] Within other Christian circles and in the evangelical tradition, this commitment has been maintained, but far too often with a loss of the comprehensive, creation-wide, public dimensions of the faith, with the result that Jesus is affirmed as savior but hardly as savior of *the world*. This is what we call the "privatization of religion," in which freedom of religion is tolerated within the private sphere of our lives but kept out of the major public spheres of life.

The result is that on the liberal side of Western Christianity, we are left with an eviscerated "gospel" that aligns itself primarily with the left wing of our culture and is constitutionally unable "to face the negative as well as the positive implication of the confession of Jesus as Lord"[4]—that is, to allow the gospel to shape and form a critique of our Western culture. Within the evangelical world, we retain a commitment to Jesus as Lord but primarily as a personal savior, so that we have little of consequence to say to a West in crisis, let alone to the Global South.

Quite naturally, but most unfortunately, this polarization manifests itself in the preaching of churches. In *I Believe in Preaching,* John Stott makes similar points to those above. He notes that liberals aim right at contemporary life in their preaching.[5] Alas, one is not always sure where sermons have come *from*! I recall some years ago participating in a gathering of practical theologians from across the UK. Two members were appointed to interpret our overall deliberations. One commented that he thought we were agreed that the Bible should not be *over us* but *alongside us* as a dialogue partner. A courageous Hebrew and Old Testament professor demurred, rightly stating that this was not the view of all of us! Clearly, if the Bible is reduced to a dialogue partner, then there is no reason why preaching should be rooted and grounded in Scripture. By comparison, evangelical sermons originate *from* the Bible, but they tend to be aimed *at* nowhere in particular. As Stott says of evangelical preaching:

> If we are conservatives ... and stand in the tradition of historic Christian orthodoxy, we live on the Bible side of the gulf. That is where we feel comfortable and safe. We believe the Bible, love the Bible, read the Bible, study the Bible and expound the Bible. But we are not at home in the modern world on the other side. ... If I were to draw a diagram of the gulf between the two worlds, and then plot our sermons on the diagram, I would have to draw a straight line which begins in the biblical world, and then goes up in the air on a straight trajectory, but never lands on the other side. For our preaching is seldom if ever earthed. It fails to build a

bridge into the modern world. It is biblical, but not contemporary.[6]

Stott characterizes this dichotomy between liberal and evangelical preaching as one of the greatest tragedies of our day:

> On the one hand, conservatives are biblical but not contemporary, while on the other liberals and radicals are contemporary but not biblical. Why must we polarize in this naïve way, however? Each side has a legitimate concern, the one to conserve God's revelation, the other to relate meaningfully to real people in the real world. Why can we not combine each other's concerns? Is it not possible for liberals to learn from conservatives the necessity of conserving the fundamentals of historic, biblical Christianity, and for conservatives to learn from liberals the necessity of relating these radically and relevantly to the real world?[7]

Stott's analysis of evangelical preaching rewards close reflection on its implications. Evangelicals pride themselves, understandably, on being "Bible Christians," and it is to their credit that they hold the Bible in such high esteem. Modernity, not least through much mainline biblical scholarship, has again and again targeted the trustworthiness of Scripture. Whether through the doctrine of inerrancy or that of infallibility, evangelicals and other orthodox Christians have by and large stood firm on the fully trustworthy nature of the Bible as holy Scripture. Personally, it was during my years at Oxford University that I realized there was a gap between the *logically* compelling nature of such doctrines and the *hermeneutical* question of how to listen to God speaking authoritatively through Scripture. How do we listen to Scripture so that we can preach the Bible for all its worth in today's world?

To return to Stott's characterization of evangelical preaching, the area of *application* is where the problems surface most clearly, for if the sermon is not aimed anywhere in particular, it is bound to hit it. The possibilities and challenge of application in preaching are summed up in the phrase, "Land the plane!" I owe this provocative metaphor comparing a sermon to flying a plane to my friend, colleague, and rector, Ray David Glenn. It is not unusual for us to discuss in the days leading up to a Sunday how to land the text we are preaching on at St. Georges the coming Sunday. Through prayer, reflection, and hard exegetical work, we may have arrived at an understanding of the text, but how do we deliver that on Sunday in our particular context so that, through the preaching, we will hear God's address to us today? How do we land the plane whose cargo is the living Word of God so that it is present and received as such by our congregations?

By the end of this book, we will have a clear idea of what is involved in "landing the plane." But to arrive there, we need to attend to several issues en route. To extend our flying metaphor, this will not be a direct flight, but the stops we make along the way will enable us to arrive more fully at our destination.

THE DESTINATION, THE PLANE, AND THE CARGO

When we read Scripture, certain passages are what I call "nodal texts." They are rich, dense, concentrated passages that, if explored carefully and fully, open up large swaths of Scripture and enable us to see the connections running through the Bible. One such "node" is Exodus 19:3-6, a passage that also nicely fits in with our flying metaphor. However, while in this passage the cargo is the people of God, in our broader metaphor of preaching as flying a plane, the cargo is the Word of God. Yahweh has rescued his people from slavery in Egypt and brought them to Mount Sinai, where he is about to establish a legally binding, covenant relationship between them and him, whereby he will be their God and they will be his people. At this poignant moment in this nodal text, Yahweh reviews what he has done for them and his plans for their future. In Exodus 19:4 Yahweh compares his rescue of the Israelites from Egypt to an eagle flying with her young on her back: "You yourselves have seen what I did to Egypt, and how I carried you on eagles' wings and brought you to myself." This is a wonderfully intimate and evocative description of the exodus. And what safer airline to fly than Air Yahweh? Indeed, Yahweh has his own airline, which since Pentecost departs *from every destination on the globe, but it only flies to one* destination! "I brought you to myself."

Here we are at the very heart of what biblical religion is about: being brought to God. He is, himself, the destination. Jesus expresses this wonderfully clearly in John 17:3: "Now this is eternal life: that they know you, the only true God, and Jesus Christ, whom you have sent." "Eternal life" is easily misunderstood as life that continues forever, a type of immortality. The life that flows from being brought to God does indeed continue forever, but "eternal life" means more than that, as I first learned years ago from Leon Morris' fine commentary on John.[8] Eternal life is the life of the age to come and will only be understood correctly when read against the background of biblical eschatology. "Eschatology" refers to the doctrine of the last things. In some circles it is used to refer to the signs of the second coming; I use it here to refer to the end times, but in the sense that with the coming of Christ the end time has already broken into history. In Jesus' day the Jews eagerly looked forward to the breaking-in of the end time, the eschaton, when God would vanquish his enemies and remove evil from creation. The New Testament assumes such a view but with a vital difference: The age to come, the kingdom of God, has already come in Jesus and will be consummated when he returns in glory. Thus, from a New Testament perspective, we are already living in the end times! The Gospel of John uses the language of "the kingdom of God" sparingly, and one of John's synonyms for it is "eternal life." Thus eternal life is far more than life that goes on forever. It is life as God intended it to be, the life of the kingdom of God, which has already broken into history and is available freely in Jesus.

As in the garden of Eden, the knowledge of God contained in eternal life is *intensely personal*. Karl Barth rightly notes that the tree of life in Genesis 2:9 is a sign of God as coinhabitant of Eden,[9] and several scholars have noted that Eden is depicted in Genesis 2–3 as a type of sanctuary.[10] The word "Eden" in the Hebrew is a play on the word for "delight," so Eden is a garden of delight. As I have noted elsewhere, "garden" is hardly the right word, since Eden is more of an extensive park.[11] The park of Eden was full of delights, but chief among them was an intimate relationship with Yahweh Elohim (NIV "Lord God"), the distinctive name of God in Genesis 2–4, to which we will return below.

In the Old Testament, the language of "to know" can be a way of expressing the intimate sexual bond of marriage. "Knowledge of God" includes knowledge *about* Yahweh— how could it be otherwise?—but is thus far more than that. It involves being brought into a personal relationship with him and, in the process, finding oneself part of the one, holy, catholic, and apostolic church, the universal people of God.

A good metaphor sparks an illuminating similarity between two unlikely things. I hope this is apparent to you from the idea of Air Yahweh! However, such a metaphor works precisely because there are so many ways in which Yahweh is unlike an airline. These dissimilarities are themselves revealing, as we have already seen in that airlines fly to many destinations, Air Yahweh to only one: himself!

Yahweh literally rescued the Israelites and literally led them to Mount Sinai. Since Pentecost God is worshiped in spirit and truth throughout the world (John 4:23-24), so it is rare—although not unknown; think of pilgrimage—for us to make a geographical journey to faith in God. We live in a later act in the great drama of Scripture, in the age of mission that fits between the coming of the kingdom and its final consummation. In our act of the drama the airline functions somewhat differently and is more appropriately rebranded as Air Trinity, though the destination is ultimately the same.

The doctrine of the Trinity emerges out of encountering the Jewish Jesus. In a monotheist context, once the disciples came to see that Jesus was indeed the Son of God, the rudiments of the doctrine of the Trinity were in place. A good place for reflecting on the rebranding of Air Yahweh as Air Trinity is John 1: "In the beginning was the Logos, and the Logos was with God, and the Logos was God. ... The Logos became flesh and made his dwelling among us."[12]

Like the outstanding preacher he was, John uses *logos* (Greek for "word," "event") in the preface to his Gospel. Hearers acquainted with Greek thought would have pricked up their ears at this point because in the ancient Greek philosophy of Heraclitus and the Stoics the *logos* was the rational principle of the universe. Similarly, a Jew hearing John 1 would never have missed the intertextual allusion to Genesis 1:1, "In the beginning…" Both groups would have been aware that something enormous was coming: the principle of the entire cosmos, that which was in the beginning of everything!

What would have utterly floored both groups is John 1:14: "The Word became flesh and made his dwelling [literally "tabernacled"—sanctuary symbolism again!] among us." For Greeks this was anathema; for Jews, the great stumbling block. For those of us who believe, it is *eternal life!* For you know as well as I do the basic content of John's Gospel— how in Christ God has acted to bring us back to him.

Much ink has been spilled over what *precisely* is meant by referring to Jesus as "the Logos."[13] In my view, its basic meaning is simple and yet profound: "The word" is the means by which we communicate with and give ourselves to one another. Think of the pathos of "Je t'aime" ("I love you") spoken in an appropriate context! Jesus is the one through whom God comes into our midst, offers himself to us, and brings us to himself.

And it is in Scripture that we find Jesus. Why do you think the early Christians in Acts 2:42 devoted themselves to the teaching of the apostles? We might have expected to read that they devoted themselves to the Old Testament Scriptures, and while this was doubtless part of the apostles' teaching, the text says that it was to the teaching of the apostles that they devoted themselves, because it was there that Jesus was to be found. I like to think of Scripture as that field in which is hid the pearl of great price, so that as we dig in this field we find ourselves brought to God again and again.

The written Word is the means God uses to bring us to himself—and he does so repeatedly. Karl Barth notes that God is by no means confined to speaking through Scripture.[14] He can speak through dreams, through nature, in our experiences, and so on. Where he so speaks, we do well to attend to him! However, as Barth observes, *within the Church* God's ordained means to speak is the Bible, the canon of holy Scripture, and all extrabiblical "speakings" must always be tested alongside Scripture. Within the church Scripture must be read, listened to, and preached, for only thus can we hope to be addressed by God and brought to him again and again.

The centrality of the Word in the congregation is wonderfully highlighted by 20th-century German missiologist Georg Vicedom. He notes, "The true shape of the congregation appears where it is clearly understood that the Word and the congregation are an indissoluble unity. They are so closely related to each other that what is said about the Word is readily applied to the congregation."[15] In support of this view, Vicedom refers to the parables of Matthew 13 and Mark 4, but especially to Acts (6:7; 12:24; 19:20), where Luke speaks of the growth of the Word when he means the growth of the congregation! As Vicedom says, "The Word itself therefore takes on a shape of its own in the congregation and becomes in the congregation a life-giving and self-propagating Word."[16]

Do you begin to see the potential and significance of preaching? Like Air Yahweh and later Air Trinity, it carries the word of God with the dynamic possibility of landing *in God*—the possibility for our lives to be grounded anew in the overwhelming reality of the living and true God. In Revelation (Rev 1:12–16), John pictures the churches as lampstands, with Jesus walking among them. His primary way of walking is through his Word, as it is read, listened to, and preached. Dr. Martyn Lloyd-Jones, one of the great preachers of the 20th century, said that he looked for preaching that ushered him into the presence of God. John Stott noted that we need truth on fire in our pulpits. The Word is the means of encounter with the living God, and the sermon is there to facilitate this encounter.

We will be returning to the sermon and the preacher throughout. Note that, flowing from what I have said above, the sermon is aimed primarily, although not exclusively, at the *hearts* of the congregation. I use "heart" here in the sense in which it is used in Old Testament Wisdom literature: to refer to the center of a person, to the part of the human person that needs to be guarded because out of it flow the issues of life (see Prov 4:23). This is not to say that *propositional* and *emotional* dimensions should be lacking, but they should not dominate the sermon. There will always be a cognitive, propositional dimension to a sermon, but a sermon is denatured when it becomes a lecture. In my experience some preachers, as they recognize the need for depth and rigor, end up transforming the sermon into a lecture aimed almost entirely at the head. Such sermons may be instructive but will not open up the whole of a person to the reality of God in an existential encounter. Similarly, emotions clearly have a part to play in preaching, but we are all too familiar with sermons dominated by endless tearjerker stories that may move us emotionally but again fail to open us up to the reality of God. Rather preaching must be directed at the congregation's hearts, for it is at this deepest level of our being that we connect with God.

THE CAPTAIN

If we think of the preacher's relationship to Air Trinity, it is unhelpful to think of the preacher as the captain of the sermon/aircraft. The Spirit is the captain. But at the same time we should not underestimate the role and huge responsibility of the preacher. Eugene Peterson comments in *The Contemplative Pastor* that it is hard to see how a pastor can lead the flock beside still waters if he or she does not live there.[17] And so too it is with the sermon: how can we copilot Air Trinity if it is not a journey we make regularly and particularly in the course of our sermon preparation? As we live with God's Word in preparation to bring it to his people, we need to find ourselves emerging again and again in his presence. The Word needs to bring us to him so that we might be a means for the Word to bring the whole congregation to him.

In this vein, Ed Stetzer reports:

> The amount of time spent in prayer and personal devotions raises questions about the vitality of many pastors' spiritual lives. While 52 percent report spending one to six hours in prayer each week, 5 percent say they spend no time at all in prayer. Furthermore, while 52 percent say they spend two to five hours a week in personal devotions unrelated to teaching preparation, 14 percent indicate they spend an hour or less in personal devotions each week.[18]

It is hard to see how such a prayer life could facilitate an ongoing pastoral ministry leading God's people ever more deeply into the very life of God. Pastors are not apostles in the unique sense in which the foundational Twelve were. But within the one, holy, catholic, and *apostolic* Church, there is an important continuity between the ministry of the apostles and the pastor/preacher. In Acts 6 we read how complaints emerged because the widows among the Grecian Jews were being overlooked in the distribution of food. The Twelve gather "all the disciples" and tell them that it would not be right for them to neglect the ministry of the Word to wait on tables. Thus the first deacons are appointed so that the apostles can devote their attention to prayer and the ministry of the Word.

Here we have the two huge landmarks of a biblical pastoral ministry: to be characterized by prayer and the ministry of the Word. In the modern pastorate there are many demands on a pastor's time. I'm not arguing that all of these are inappropriate—take counseling, for example. Sixteenth-century Reformer Ulrich Zwingli rightly saw that this is part of the ministry of the Word. In my experience, preaching and one-on-one discipleship and spiritual direction go hand in hand. In preaching one brings God's Word to the whole congregation, endeavoring to feed the giants and the newborn babes in Christ—no easy challenge! In spiritual direction one walks alongside an individual seeking to discern what God is doing and saying in his or her life. Thus prayer and the ministry of the Word must not be defined too narrowly or individualistically.

However, we are in deep trouble when prayer and devotion to the ministry of the Word are not front and center in the pastorate. Our consumer culture fosters a real temptation to think that if we just get the formula right, we can manage a healthy church into existence, and there are countless books and groups that will help you do this. Indeed, Eugene Peterson starts his excellent *Working the Angles* by reporting that pastors are leaving the ministry in droves in America. They are not leaving their churches, but are transforming their churches into businesses!

> American pastors are abandoning their posts,
> left and right, and at an alarming rate. They
> are not leaving their churches and getting oth-
> er jobs. ... But they are abandoning their posts,
> their calling. They have gone whoring after
> other gods. What they do with their time under
> the guise of pastoral ministry hasn't the remot-
> est connection with what the church's pastors
> have done for most of the twenty centuries. ...
> The pastors of America have metamorphosed
> into a company of shopkeepers, and the shops
> they keep are churches.[19]

Instead of prayer and the Word taking up the major time
and energy of the pastor, they become marginal or non-
existent as the machinery of church growth is set in
place and then maintained and oiled so that it functions
as a slick, expertly run organization. This is like a pilot
serving drinks and meals and chatting away to passen-
gers—wonderful things in and of themselves—while ne-
glecting the task of flying the plane, which he or she alone
is trained to do. The life of every church *does* include an or-
ganizational aspect, and this dimension ought to be done
well, but the point of Acts 6 is that this is where the gifts of
other wise and Spirit-filled Christians come into play.

In his autobiography, *The Pastor*, Peterson tells of how
he nearly came to resign from his church.[20] The reason:
too many meetings, which kept him from the Word and
prayer. His elders responded beautifully: let us take care
of the meetings and you get on with your primary duties.
Intriguingly, he narrates how hard he found it to let go of
the meetings, continuing to show up at them until challenged by his elders not to do so!

Meetings are tangible; minutes are produced, and one
can point to business achieved. Prayer and devotion to

the Word are hidden; like our Father, they are "in secret" or "unseen" (Matt 6:6). This is their glory—but sadly, it is rare for governing bodies of churches to evaluate pastors in such terms. Imagine an annual evaluation where a pastor was asked to report how often he or she was aboard Air Trinity! Do we ever inquire of pastors whether they regularly go on retreat? Have you ever attended a meeting where concern is expressed over whether pastors get enough time for such activities?

A good sign of our times is that through the work of Eugene Peterson, Joyce Huggett, Margaret Silf, and many others, the practices of prayer are being recovered. The Protestant tradition is not overwhelmed with resources in this respect, and evangelicals are appropriating the practices of silence, contemplation, Ignatian styles of prayer, spiritual direction, *lectio divina*, and so on from our Catholic brothers and sisters. When this is done healthily, the Word remains central to such renewal, as it must.

I haven't been able to track down the source of this quote, but I believe it was once said that we "need to give prayer back to the Church." There is no chance of this if our leaders are not themselves men and women of prayer and the Word. I often tell my students two things about the pastoral ministry: (1) At its best there is nothing quite like it. It is a rich, rewarding and wonderfully fulfilling vocation. (2) The experience of the pastorate from the inside is quite different from when viewed from the outside. The pastorate is *intensely public*; week after week one is in the pulpit preaching the Word. There are days when there is nothing you want to do more, and there are days when you would run from it if you could! How can one possibly sustain such a life unless one is living ever more deeply and wisely into the very life of God?

On reflection, the appointment of a pastor by a church is a very strange thing. All Christians are full-time servants of God (cf. Rom 12:1-2), so why appoint a pastor? Peterson has it right in my view: The sheep—amid their diverse and demanding callings—appoint the pastor *to keep them attentive to God!*[21] The main means of this are prayer and the ministry of the Word. As every minister sooner or later discovers, one has to shepherd the sheep while living one's own life and holding it together. No easy task, but it is impossible if we ourselves are not attentive to God on a daily basis.

THE VIEW FROM ARRIVALS

Arriving at an airport is never the end of the journey. With Air Trinity it might seem like it, but once we explore the view from arrivals, it becomes clear that far more awaits us.

As one who flies a fair bit, I cannot say that airports evoke delight in me. Apart from surviving a particularly turbulent flight, it would never occur to me to kiss the ground on disembarking the plane. It's totally different with Air Trinity: There is always only one destination, and the view is magnificent. One is overwhelmed by the reality of the true and living God: the hunter, the warrior, the king; the God who approaches at infinite speed. Awe, love, holiness, and mystery combine to make arrivals the purpose of the journey.

So majestic is the view that one is tempted, like Peter on the Mount of Transfiguration, to say, "Let's camp here and soak in the view."[22] Like Peter, we rightly say, "Master, it is good to be here!" (Luke 9:33). And it is! However, there is more to the view from arrivals than our experience of it

being good. Peter is so overwhelmed by the vision of Jesus
in his glory that he proposes staying put there: "Let us put
up three shelters—one for you, one for Moses and one for
Elijah" (Luke 9:33). In the process Peter is in danger of miss-
ing the significance of the transfiguration, unlike Moses
and Elijah, the great figureheads of the Old Testament
Law and the Prophets, who discussed with Jesus his "exodus," which he was to bring to fulfillment in Jerusalem.
The Glorious One is on a journey to lead the whole creation
in an exodus from sin and bondage, and Peter's comment
is, "Let's stay here!" Little wonder that in one of his narrative asides, Luke comments, "He did not know what he was
saying" (Luke 9:33).

Air Yahweh brings us to Yahweh—or, as Paul might put
it, we find ourselves "in Christ." It is worth reflecting on
Yahweh, the dominant name for God in the Old Testament.
It is above all the name of the redeemer God who rescues
Israel from slavery and brings it to himself (see Exod 3; 6).
The name speaks of God as the covenant God who says
to Israel, "I will be your God and you will be my people."
However, the Old Testament makes it crystal-clear that
Yahweh the redeemer is also creator, and thus his redemp-
tive purposes always include his purposes for his creation
as a whole.

In Genesis 1:1–2:3, the ancient Near Eastern gener-
ic name for God, *elohim*, is used throughout the passage.
In Genesis 2:4–24, as humankind enters the story with
its relationality, God's name changes to the unusual com-
bination of "Yahweh *elohim*." Theologically, this is highly
significant. The relational God of the covenant, Yahweh,
is the creator God, *elohim*. Further, as Bill Dumbrell
has shown, detailed study of the covenants of the Old
Testament reveals that Genesis 1 is the foundational covenant text. Covenant in the Old Testament, and kingdom in

the New, are not "just" about individual salvation and the Church, although they are certainly that, but also about God's purpose to lead his entire creation to liberation until it is transformed into the new heavens and the new earth.[23] And Yahweh/Jesus is the agent of this cosmic redemption.

Upon arrival, we doubtless are tempted to sing the well-known chorus from Helen Howarth Lemmel's hymn:

> Turn your eyes upon Jesus,
> look full in his wonderful face,
> and the things of earth
> will grow strangely dim
> in the light of his glory and grace.

I think I understand the intent of this much-loved song, but it is in danger of a Platonic, otherworldly worldview that denigrates the earthly in relation to the "spiritual." It would, I suggest, be more biblical to sing something like:

> Turn your eyes upon Jesus,
> look full in his wonderful face,
> and the things of the earth
> *take their rightful place*
> in the light of his glory and grace.[24]

To encounter Yahweh is never to be turned away from the world, but to be turned toward the world *as his creation*— his "footstool," in biblical terms (Isa 66:1; Acts 7:49; Matt 5:35). Creation is by no means to be equated with God, but it does have great dignity and value as his handiwork. To encounter Jesus Christ is to encounter Jesus the Messiah, the King. And over what realm does he rule but the entire creation? In the New Testament the Church is central to the kingdom of God; it is a sign of the kingdom, but it must never be equated with the kingdom. The kingdom is bigger and more extensive in its relationship to God's recovery of his purposes through Jesus for his entire creation.

David Broughton Knox, former principal of Moore Theological Seminary and George Whitefield College, where I taught, once poignantly captured this insight when he said to me that when we gather around Christ, he stands with his face to his world! The view at arrivals is centered on God, but precisely because this is its center it takes in the vista of the whole of creation. It is a bigger view than we often imagine. In our preaching, the *King* must be front and center, but precisely as he is front and center, the whole of creation will come into view as the *kingdom* to which he lays claim. It cannot be otherwise.

Another way of putting this is that when we encounter God as Yahweh, when we encounter Jesus as the Messiah, we discover who we are *and* the true nature, the true story, of our world. Occasionally in history a new convert appears who sees this immediately; most of us are more like Peter.

Perhaps the greatest Christian thinker of the 18th century was German philosopher Johann Georg Hamann (1730-1788). Although interest in his work is reviving, he is not nearly as well known as he should be. Hamann studied at the University of Königsberg, where he embraced the Enlightenment spirit of his day. After graduating he worked for the firm of a family friend. He was sent on a diplomatic mission to London that went disastrously wrong; so too did Hamann's life, and eventually he found himself in a hotel room, desperate and alone, with his money running out. He got ahold of a Bible. Initially it had no impact on him, but he tried again and was thoroughly converted. What is so fascinating about Hamann's conversion is that he immediately saw that the Bible does two things: (1) It explains ourselves to ourselves, and (2) it explains the true character of the world to us.

When he returned to Königsberg, Hamann's firm welcomed him back, but it was deeply concerned about his faith and sought the help of a prominent young philosopher at the University of Königsberg, Immanuel Kant (1724–1804), to try to reconvert Hamann to the faith of the Enlightenment. It was Hamann's insight into what the Bible does that enabled him to take on the Enlightenment at its roots. Before Kant had even published his first *Critique*, Hamann had written what some regard as the most penetrating critique of it.

Hamann understood the "view from arrivals" and thus was able to do truly penetrating missional work in the world of his day. His grasp of what the Bible *does*, and not just what it *is*, enabled him to facilitate a deep encounter between the gospel and Enlightenment culture. In my phrasing, he understood that the Bible tells the true story of the whole world.[25]

A story will illustrate what this means. After some time living in India as a missionary, Lesslie Newbigin was challenged by a well-educated Hindu friend who said to him:

> As I read the Bible I find in it a quite unique interpretation of universal history and, therefore, a unique understanding of the human person as a responsible actor in history. You Christian missionaries have talked of the Bible as it were simply another book of religion. We have plenty of these already in India and we do not need another to add to our supply.[26]

As Newbigin's friend points out, what is unique about the Bible is that it is universal history; in other words, it tells the true story of the whole world. Jewish literary scholar Erich Auerbach also gets at this in his classic, *Mimesis*, in which he refers to the "totalitarian" nature of the Bible: it overwhelms us and insists that its version of reality is the true one.[27] Connected to a welcome recovery of the importance of narrative in philosophy, theology, missiology, and many other disciplines is the insight that our lives only make sense in terms of the narrative of which they are a part. Our worldviews are grounded at their deepest level in metanarratives or grand, comprehensive stories about the world. Narrative provides an exceptionally fertile means to understand what the Bible *does*. We know it is the fully trustworthy Word of God, but how does it function as such? What does it do? There are few more important questions for the church and, especially, the preacher. Through the lens of narrative or story—not to be confused with thinking that the Bible is thus "unhistorical"—the Bible should be seen as the book that tells the true story of the whole world.

In one sense, this is not so obvious. The Bible is a collection of 66 (or 73, if you are Catholic) books—a kind of library. In this sense I like to think of the Bible as a deposit—like the silt that a river leaves behind as it flows over many kilometers through diverse landscape—of God's journey with Israel, culminating in the Christ event. In another sense it is so obvious that the Bible tells the story from creation to new creation that we easily overlook this important insight. In Peterson's words, the Bible is a grand, sprawling, capacious metanarrative.[28] It has an overarching, storied shape to it, and it is essential to take this into account if we wish to grasp Scripture in its totality and be grasped by Scripture in its totality—what is called *tota Scriptura*.

Grasping Scripture in its unity and being grasped by it really is of tremendous importance today. Scottish theologian James Orr (1844–1913) and Dutch polymath Abraham Kuyper (1837–1920) contemporaneously realized that modernity operates out of a unified vision for all of life that could only be responded to by a similarly unified Christian worldview.[29] Such a worldview needs to be authorized by a unified view of the Bible, and a narrative reading of the Bible as a whole is an indispensable resource in this respect. Evangelicals have played an important role in keeping the Bible central to the life of the church, but alas, often in a fragmented, piecemeal way. Within mainline denominations the lectionary approach has not been much better, with very little sense of the overarching metanarrative fed into the life of the church. The church calendar has immense potential in this regard, but once again, in practice it is hard to find the grand sweep from creation through to new creation.

It is vital to note that as a grand story Scripture tells not just the story of the Church but the story of the world, of which the church forms a central part. Thus a narrative approach to the Bible as a whole alerts us to:

- the unified story of the Bible
- the story as the story *of the whole world*
- this story as *the true story* of the whole world

Each of these elements is vital if we are to grasp what the Bible does.

The Unified Story of the Bible

Analysis of the Bible as a drama in five or six acts has proved fertile in recent years.[30] Michael Goheen and I propose we think of the Bible as a drama in six acts:

1. **God Establishes the Kingdom:** Creation
2. **Rebellion in the Kingdom:** Fall

3. **The King Chooses Israel:** Redemption Initiated
   - A People for the King
   - A Land and a King for God's People

Interlude: A Kingdom Story Waiting for an Ending: The Intertertestamental Period

4. **The Coming of the King:** Redemption Accomplished
5. **Spreading the News of the King:** The Mission of the Church
   - From Jerusalem to Rome
   - And into All the World
6. **The Return of the King:** Redemption Completed

The drama of the Bible alerts us to the fascinating way in which God has chosen to reveal himself and to bring salvation to the world. God did not reveal from heaven, for example, the Thirty-Nine Articles (Anglican) or the Heidelberg Catechism (Reformed), much as we rightly revere such documents. Instead he formed a people and immersed himself in the life of the ancient Near Eastern nation of Israel. This is what we mean when we speak of God's progressive revelation; it is given over many years *in history*. Israel was an ancient Near Eastern nation, and its literature bears all the marks of that cultural context. Its law is ancient Near Eastern law, albeit with important distinctives. Its form of worship was focused in a typically ancient Near Eastern way on a tabernacle and then a temple, albeit with some very important differences.

As part of Scripture the literature of act 3 remains authoritative for us today, but the difference between act 3 and act 5 has to be taken into account as we listen to such literature for God's address. Tom Wright's analogy of an imagined discovery of an incomplete play by Shakespeare, given to actors who have to improvise from all they know of Shakespeare's works and from the incomplete manuscript to act out the drama today, is helpful.[31] It alerts us to the hard work involved in preaching!

On the one hand the story of Scripture is wonderfully illuminating. It provides us with a hermeneutic for understanding the world and clearly shows us where we as the church fit in the grand story. We also know how the story will end. Theologically, we can relate this to the clarity of Scripture. The landmark events and truths are clearly presented and do not require biblical scholars and language specialists to be understood. But "clarity" is a metaphor, and the reverse side of this metaphor is that much in Scripture is unclear. We live in act 5, and not acts 1–3 or 6. But all these other acts bear on act 5, and the preacher is called to do the hard work of discerning how these acts continue to inform and govern our lives today. At the same time act 4 is the center of the Bible, and the Christ event casts its light backward and forward. The Christ event cannot be understood apart from acts 1–3, but it is also explosive news, radically new and unexpected.

This, incidentally, is a reason why God's full-time servants set aside those gifted in preaching and the ministry of the Word. Preachers and pastors are set aside to devote themselves to Scripture so that they can make increasingly clear what is unclear in Scripture; this enables the church to appropriate more and more fully the whole counsel of God today. The seriousness and challenge of this task should not be underestimated.

I think Brevard Childs was right in his view that "unity and diversity" is an unhelpful way of thinking about Scripture, since ultimately Scripture is God's Word, and he speaks with a unified voice.[32] However, the Bible is historically and culturally diverse and specific, and this kind of diversity has to be taken into account if we are to read it rightly.

This is true even of passages that can easily be read directly from the Old Testament into our situation today. Take the first commandment, for example: "You shall have no other gods before me" (Exod 20:2; Deut 5:7). I think it is right to understand this commandment as, first, prohibiting the presence of other gods—what the Old Testament calls *idols*—in the tabernacle or temple "next to" Yahweh. The presence of multiple gods in a temple would have been common in the ancient Near East, but this is forbidden by Yahweh as he establishes a covenant relationship with his people at Sinai. In this way any type of syncretistic worship is strictly forbidden among God's people. We know from the history of Israel that this was a real temptation again and again. But what does it mean for us today? We are not generally tempted to worship Baal, Molech, or any of the other ancient Near Eastern deities. The preacher will need to work out what this norm for being God's people means in our contexts today. We will say more about this below.

The Bible as the Story of the Whole World

Application of the Bible always takes place in a context. The largest context in which it takes place is that of the world. The Bible tells the true story of the world and thus provides us with indispensable clues about the context in which we preach today.

The Bible is, first, God's Word to God's people. Just as in one form of Communion liturgy the leader proclaims, "The gifts of God for the people of God," before distributing the bread and the wine, so too the Bible is God's Word for God's people. In this sense the church is the primary place for the reception of Scripture. But this decidedly does *not* mean that the story the Bible tells is "just" about the church.

Twentieth-century Christianity has been plagued with dualisms in its understanding of the relationship between redemption/salvation and creation. However, if we begin the biblical story where the Bible begins, then we cannot but take God as creator and the whole of his creation with the utmost seriousness. Gordon Spykman notes that evangelical Christians have been so quick to move to belief in the second article of the Apostles' Creed—Christ—that they often bypass belief in the first, namely creation. He speaks in this respect of an eclipse of the doctrine of creation in evangelicalism.[33] The problem with such an eclipse is that without a robust doctrine of creation we will inevitably misunderstand the cross and redemption.

Beginning where the Bible begins compels us to take God's creation of the world seriously and to ask how act 1 of the drama of the Bible relates to the other acts. Does the fall, for example, mean that God gives up on his purposes for creation and concentrates on saving souls? If not—and I certainly think not!—then how does redemption relate to creation?

This is where narrative and biblical theology are of great import. In the Old Testament the most helpful way into the relationship between creation and redemption is via a theology of covenant.[34] The first use of the word "covenant" (*berit*) occurs in Genesis 6:18, in the context of the covenant with Noah. Dumbrell has shown how this refers back to the creation covenant. In Genesis 12:1-3 the word "bless" in one form or another occurs five times, countering the word "curse," which appears in one form or another six times in Genesis 1-11 (Gen 3:14, 17; 4:11; 5:29; 8:21; 9:25). The message is clear: God is going to recover his purpose of blessing for his entire creation through Abraham and his descendants. The call and election of Abraham is never viewed as an end in itself but as a means to bring blessing to the nations. All of this theology needs to be in view when we encounter the description of Jesus as the "son of Abraham" in the New Testament (Matt 1:1; Luke 3:33).

Within the New Testament a major clue to the relationship between creation and redemption is in the main theme of Jesus' teaching—namely, the kingdom of God/heaven. Kingdom is all about the reign of Israel's God over the entire creation, and the New Testament reshapes Jewish hopes about the future (eschatology) by declaring that in Christ the kingdom has already come and that it will be consummated at the end of history when Christ returns to usher in the new heavens and the new earth. The Church is a sign of the kingdom, but the kingdom as the reign of God is far bigger than the Church. In the hymn of Philippians 2 Paul captures the comprehensiveness of what is in view in Philippians 2:10-11: "that at the name of Jesus every knee should bow, in heaven and on earth and under the earth, and every tongue acknowledge that Jesus Christ is Lord, to the glory of God the Father."

In terms of Christology, it is important to note that Jesus' preferred self-designation is "Son of Man," a term found mainly on Jesus' lips in the Gospels and not much used outside them. Jesus, in my view, deliberately chose this expression rather than "messiah" since the latter was too explosive in his context, and he only "comes out" clearly and publicly as the Messiah once he is ready to catalyze the opposition to him that will trigger the events leading to the cross. "Son of Man" has two major allusions to the Old Testament: first in Ezekiel, where it means humankind in humankind's weakness, and then in Daniel 7, where a truly regal figure is in view. In Daniel 7 the "one like a son of man" "was given authority, glory and sovereign power; all nations and peoples of every language worshiped him. His dominion is an everlasting dominion that will not pass away, and his kingdom is one that will never be destroyed" (Dan 7:14). Daniel 7 is the primary background for understanding Jesus' understanding of himself and the view is of him as King over all.

How, one might ask, is the church a sign of the kingdom of Jesus over all? In Mark (see Mark 10:17-31), a synonym for "becoming a Christian" or "[being] saved" (Mark 10:26) is "[entering] the kingdom" (Mark 10:23-25). Christians are those who have already actively embraced the kingship of Jesus, so the Church is *already* the place where every knee bows before King Jesus and every tongue confesses that Jesus is Lord. Little wonder that when Jesus taught his disciples to pray, he included: "Your kingdom come on earth as it is in heaven." Similarly, Paul uses the delightful expression "the obedience of faith" (Rom 1:5; 16:26 ESV).

In Ephesians 1:10 Paul speaks of God's plan "to bring unity to all things in heaven and on earth under Christ." Perhaps one of the most fertile passages in which we find the relationship between redemption and creation articulated is Colossians 1:15-20: Christ is "the head of the body, the church" (Col 1:18), and this same Christ is "the firstborn over all creation" (Col 1:15). Acts 3:15 poignantly describes Jesus as the "author of life," and Revelation 11:15 jubilantly proclaims when the seventh angel sounds his trumpet: "The kingdom of the world has become the kingdom of our Lord and of his Messiah, and he will reign for ever and ever."

Clearly the gospel is not just personal and individual truth—although it certainly is this—but also public truth. The Old Testament is of vital importance in this respect, alerting us as it does that being in covenant with God has implications for all areas of life. Yahweh's *torah*, his instruction, is comprehensive, dealing not just with religious life, but also with family, marriage, relationship to one's neighbor, sexuality, hygiene, food, land, justice, politics, economics, and so on. Similarly, Old Testament Wisdom literature deals with the smorgasbord of human existence. One example is the Proverbs 31 woman. She is described as "a woman who fears Yahweh" (Prov 31:30 LEB), but in the history of interpretation commentators have struggled to see how this relates to all the "secular" activities connected to her, such as homemaking, trading in fabrics, buying a field and planting a vineyard, and so on.[35] What they miss is that her reverence for Yahweh manifested itself in *all* these dimensions of her human life and not just in her "spiritual" activities.

The Old Testament is chock-full of politics (see, for example, 1–2 Kings), and the prophets indict Israel for its behavior not just in organized religion but in all of life. The book of Revelation, too, contains cutting economic and political critique.[36] Abraham Kuyper famously expressed this comprehensive vision of the Bible in his statement, "There is not a square inch in the whole domain of our human existence over which Christ, who is Sovereign over *all*, does not cry: 'Mine!' "[37]

The view from arrivals is comprehensive and, thus, so too will be biblical preaching. Oliver O'Donovan, for example, in his *Desire of the Nations*, a political theology, rightly notes that theology must be political if it is to be evangelical.[38] He says that while the preacher may make the journey from the Bible to contemporary Iraq in 30 minutes, that same journey may engage a scholar for his or her lifetime. The point is that the journey must be made! God is author and ruler of all of life, and his Word is utterly comprehensive in its scope and range. If in our preaching we are sounding the kingdom note, then there is not an area of contemporary life that will be left untouched. This is not to suggest either that (1) the journey to contemporary life from the Bible is always an easy and simple one, or (2) that the preacher is called to be an expert in all areas of life.

We have already noted that the Bible with its grand story provides us with a hermeneutic for understanding ourselves and our world. Lesslie Newbigin rightly encouraged us to indwell the biblical story so that it becomes our default mode amid the challenges and temptations of the many other narratives that our culture offers us. We need to be at home in the biblical story so that it truly is *our* story. The biblical story needs to become the lens through which we interpret our world. We know the beginning and the end of the story of the world; we know what the problem is with the world, and we know the solution. However, that is not the same as saying we can always move directly from the Bible to contemporary issues in a simplistic way. We live in the same world as the Bible, God's world, but his world is historical through and through, and we live at a different time and place in history than the biblical writers.

Politically, for example, none of the biblical writers ever encountered democracy as a model for governing a nation. Even the nation-state is a modern invention. In the Old Testament, where we have the fullest political data, Israel is a theocracy, a nation in covenant with Yahweh. The church remains a theocracy, but it is not a nation; instead, it is scattered throughout all nations. Indeed, James Dunn in his commentary on Romans suggests that in Romans 13 Paul is wrestling with what an approach to government looks like in what I call act 5 of the true story.[39]

The Bible addresses the whole of life, but relating it to all of life is complex, and preachers ought to beware of naïve contemporary applications. Does the Bible address the issue of poverty? Certainly! But how does this relate to poverty today? Not an easy issue. In his magisterial *Through the Eye of a Needle*, Peter Brown examines the church's attitude towards wealth in AD 350–550.[40] It is fascinating to see how the church interacted with its culture to bring a biblical ethic to the issue of the poor and wealth. Similarly, there is a wealth of material in the Protestant Reformers on social issues and the church. All of this alerts us that when we move from the Bible to contemporary issues, we need never begin *de novo*. We inherit 2,000-plus years of tradition in this regard, and we need to be familiar with that tradition if we are not to repeat the errors of bygone ages.

At the same time, our age has its own issues, and we will need to be rigorous in working through these issues to bring a Scriptural perspective to bear on them. Take the issue of gay marriage, for example. In my view, it is clear from Scripture that sex is a gift for full expression within a heterosexual marriage bond. Thus we should neither recommend nor promote homosexual behavior, adultery, or premarital sex. With many other forms of behavior, homosexual practice falls under what the Bible calls sin or rebellion against God. However, being clear on this is a long way from knowing how to relate to the issue of gay marriage in a pluralistic, democratic nation. In Israel adultery merited the death penalty; I doubt many of us would propose such a penalty be enacted in a contemporary nation. In Israel worshiping other gods was a heinous offense also meriting the death penalty. Again, we should not go in this direction legislatively today!

These are complex issues, but to cut to the chase, I suggest we might find ourselves in a position where we do what we can to protect the civil rights of gays and lesbians while never making the mistake of advocating such practices. So too with Islam. Allah is not the Trinitarian God, but I for one want to protect the rights of Muslims to co-exist and practice their faith within a Western democracy such as the United States or Canada. At the same time predominantly Muslim countries need to be pressured to grant similar freedoms to religious minorities in their countries. I would not recommend to a person to become a Muslim, but that is a very different thing from how to relate to Islam politically and socially today.

All of this is to say that there is a hermeneutical ecology in the move from Scripture to our world today. The father of contemporary philosophical hermeneutics is German philosopher Hans-Georg Gadamer. Central to his hermeneutics is the question of how we come to understanding. In relation to texts Gadamer distinguishes between the horizon of the text and the horizon of the reader. Understanding occurs when there is a fusion of the horizons. One of Gadamer's central insights is that the reader(s) is as embedded in history as the text. He proposes a dialogical process of understanding whereby we bring our prejudices (prejudgments) and questions to the text, which opens up a dialogue that moves toward a fusion of horizons.

When hermeneutics first made inroads into the Christian community, the joke was that "Herman Neutics" was the name of a German theologian! Hopefully our discussion above has made progress toward demystifying this important discipline. While there is a beautiful simplicity to faith and to faithful reception of Scripture, our interpretation of the Bible should never become *simplistic*. J. B. Phillips wrote a book with the instructive title *Your God Is Too Small*. Alas, I fear this is often the case in our handling of the Bible. Our God is the creator-redeemer God, the God who dwells in unapproachable light. Every aspect of our creation owes its origin and maintenance in existence to him, and our responsibility as preachers is to represent him well, to enhance his reputation among God's people and in our world. Good preaching is hard work; it involves blood, sweat, and tears. Simplistic familiarity with and preaching of Scripture is the great enemy of what we need.

We have insisted above that Scripture is the story of the whole world and that it is authoritative for all of life. However, this needs to be carefully understood. It is possible to expect too much from Scripture when we look to it to provide answers that it is not designed to provide. I sometimes give my students the example of counseling those who have suffered the trauma of rape. Nowhere in Scripture will you find a theory of rape counseling, and pastors can do real damage if they rush into the trauma of rape with Bible in hand but no understanding of the empirical effects of rape. Scripture teaches all sorts of things that a good theory for such counseling ignores at its peril, but there is no shortcut to knowing through experience and study what happens to a person who is raped. For example, it is not uncommon for a rape victim to feel guilty, as though somehow responsible for causing the rape. Simplistic counseling—asking questions such as, "Are you trusting God in this?," "Are you having your quiet time?," and so on (and these do get asked!)—can increase that sense of guilt rather than opening a process toward healing and wholeness.

In our use of Scripture, we need to navigate the path between biblicism, in which there is a proof text for every situation, and dualism, in which the Bible is taken to have nothing to do with contemporary issues. The Bible orients us authoritatively toward the world in the sense of a worldview. On some issues—family life, for example—it does provide detailed instruction, which needs to be taken with full seriousness. Generally, however, the Bible functions at the deep, orientational level rather than at the level of specifics regarding every situation.

Hence, a preacher is *not* required to be an expert on every issue congregation members are facing! There is no reason, for example, why a preacher should be the expert on how to run a business in a given location in 2015 so that it bears witness to the reign of King Jesus in ways appropriate to healthy business. That is the responsibility of businesspeople. What a preacher *does* need to do is continually to alert those businesspeople that they are called to live under and bear witness to the reign of Jesus in this area of life. All Christians are in full-time service of the Lord Christ; the only difference is *where* we are called to serve. And the role of the pastor/preacher is to keep us attentive to God in the midst of all the challenges of contemporary life.

What the preacher will need is as deep a sense as possible of what "time" it is in our culture. John Stott spoke evocatively of the need for double listening: one ear to the Bible and one to our culture, so that in our preaching we create a bridge between the two. George Weigel noted of John Paul II that he scouted the future so as to best guide the church in the present.[41] If we think of the sermon in terms of landing a plane, then we always land it in a specific place and time, and the landing will vary from place to place. Pilots tell us that it is vital to know about the airport where you are landing: Some allow for a long, low approach, while others require a steep descent from above.

The Bible as *the True Story* of the Whole World

Below we will move on to the importance of understanding our context if we wish to land the sermon. For now we return to the third of our three points about a narrative approach to the Bible, namely that the story the Bible tells is not just any story but *the true story of the world*. A narrative approach is very useful in dialogue with those of other beliefs since we can compare the biblical story with the stories that other systems tell. What we are *not* free to do is to make the biblical story merely one among many. Lesslie Newbigin rightly points out:

> A proposal for a unity which includes both Christianity and other religions rests (openly or covertly) upon belief in some reality other than God's revelation in Christ. The experience of learning to listen to one another which the ecumenical movement has given us is certainly valid beyond the confines of Christendom. We have indeed to learn to enter into real conversation with men of other religions if they are to apprehend Jesus Christ as Saviour and if we are to learn the manifold wisdom of God which he set forth in Jesus. But the ecumenical movement remains missionary through and through because it is a movement not for any kind of unity, but for that unity which is God's creation through the lifting up of Jesus Christ upon the Cross and through the continuing work of his Spirit.[42]

Of course, it is important how we maintain and proclaim the Bible as the true story of the world. Truth in the Bible is first of all *a person*, and it is of little value if we assert the truth of the Bible while failing to embody it in becoming Christlike. One of the great missiologists of the 20th century, South African David Bosch, says that there are two things that Christians need to prioritize in our postmodern culture: worldview and plausibility structure.[43] "Plausibility structure" refers to a lived reality as a backdrop against which our words resonate and compel a hearing. One thinks, for example, of Mother Teresa going to the White House and lambasting her audience over the issue of abortion. You and I could not do that. How was it that she was able to and to be heard? The answer, of course, was her life. Her life spoke so loudly that she simply had to be listened to.

We should not take it for granted that we and our congregations know and indwell the biblical story. Hard and creative work are required to entrench an understanding of the Bible as a grand story in the life of a congregation. An example is Chris Gonzalez, a pastor in Phoenix. Chris has developed a series of icons for each act in the drama and multiple creative ways of really letting the drama of Scripture take root in his congregation. I myself developed an expanded version of the Apostles' Creed to elaborate on the storied dimension of the Bible and Christian confession (see the appendix at the end of this book).

As typical moderns we often make the mistake of thinking that if we understand something, we've got it! However, even when such understanding is in place, there is a world of difference between *understanding* that the Bible is the true story of the world and intentionally thinking and *living* out of that story. In our pluralist world proclamation of the truth of the Bible will fall on deaf ears if our lives do not provide a plausible backdrop against which we proclaim the message of the Bible.

THE AIRPORT: CONTEXTUALIZATION

The Old Testament prophets are instructive when it comes to preaching. Modern-day preachers are *not* prophets in the Old Testament sense, but there is continuity between Old Testament prophecy and preaching, and there is much we can learn from them. When you read the Old Testament prophetic books you will note that they invariably begin by locating the prophet in his particular era and geographical context (cf., e.g., Jer 1:1–3). We should also remember that the Old Testament prophets are primarily *forth*-tellers rather than *fore*-tellers. They are commissioned to convey God's Word to his people at a specific time and place. What we must learn from this is that God's Word, his address, is *always* contextual, related intimately to the specific conditions on the ground. This is what missiologists refer to as *contextualization*.

If we ignore this we will end up telling the rich young ruler he needs to be born again, and Nicodemus to sell everything and come follow Jesus. Scripture *is* fixed as a closed canon, but its application is *not*, and the context in which we preach will shape how we apply Scripture. Indeed, as I will explain below, we land the plane successfully when we preach the message shaped by *the intersection* of two trajectories: the intersection of the *telos*, or message of the text, and the context *in* which and *to* which we are preaching.

Just as we need to be intimately acquainted with Scripture, so too we need to know the context in which we preach extremely well. We can envisage the context of our preaching in relation to a series of concentric circles:

1. The creation
2. Act 5 of the biblical story
3. The 21st century AD
4. The West, Two-Thirds World, or wherever we find ourselves
5. Our particular culture(s)
6. Our congregation

The first and second circles remind us that Scripture provides us with a hermeneutic for understanding our

Bridging the gap between Scripture and culture

EXCELLENT PREACHING

Your congregation

Your specific culture

The area you live in

The time you live in

Your place in the biblical story

Creation

world and thus provides us with major presuppositions for any contextualization of the Bible's message. The world is God's good but fallen and being-redeemed creation, and God's dynamic but fixed order for his creation holds throughout history. This is important because although the biblical writers lived a long time ago and in very different places and cultures from ours, they all lived in the same world we do—namely, in God's creation. From this perspective the similarities far outweigh the differences, and we ought never to make the modern mistake of absolutizing our culture, as though history leads to its climax in us! Wedding ourselves to the spirit of the age ensures we will be widowed in the ages that follow, if not well before then. In so many ways the struggles of the biblical writers are our struggles, and thus, for example, we should not be surprised to find kindred spirits in the Psalter whose experiences resonates with ours. This continuity in history is also the reason why we can often read directly from Scripture into our own context. We may need to work out exactly what the Ten Commandments mean by "You shall not murder" and "You shall not commit adultery," but the difficulty is far more in obeying these commands than in understanding them.

Second: So much needs to be said about our being in act 5 of the drama of Scripture. We are not a theocratic nation in covenant with God, as was Old Testament Israel. The new Israel is now scattered throughout the nations as the global people of God. Act 5 is quintessentially the era of mission, and one can encapsulate the calling of God's people in act 5 as witness in word and deed. We live in the age of mission, even as we eagerly anticipate the return of Christ. Thus when we preach from acts 1–3 and 6 of the Bible, we will need to relate those acts to our lives in act 5. The Gospels and Letters were written in act 5, and thus, not surprisingly, it is generally far easier to relate them to the church today than it is to relate parts of the Old Testament.

Third: We also must bear in mind that we live in the 21st century AD. The New Testament was written in the 1st century AD, and the Old Testament was produced over several centuries BC, concluding in the postexilic period. Historically and culturally there is a big gap between the 1st century AD and the 21st, and preachers will need to be aware of this as they facilitate a bridge between Scripture and our context.

When Mike Goheen and I wrote *Living at the Crossroads: An Introduction to Christian Worldview*, we concluded the book with a series of cameos on what a Christian worldview might mean today for business, economics, politics, the arts, and so on. I remember being struck, when writing those sections, just how crucial a historical perspective is in developing a Christian approach to business, politics, and so on today. To take just one example, the Bible has much to say about economics, but we live on the other side of the Industrial Revolution and are now in the midst of the technological revolution. The science that has facilitated this is a major component of modernity, so that what we mean by business and economics cannot be simplistically read into the Bible and then back into our context today.

Fourth: I am assuming that most readers of this book live in the West or in westernized contexts. Urbanization is one of the great characteristics of our day, as is globalization, so that that there is hardly a country in the world not influenced by the West. At the same time peasants constitute a major percentage of the world's population, and a great concern of Christians should be the underdeveloped countries of the world.[44] Preaching in such contexts is as— if not more!—important than preaching in the West, and whatever our context, we need to know it well to preach well. Furthermore, we are increasingly in a global context, so that the North needs to attend to the South and the South to the North if we are to have any chance of understanding our contexts, since they are interrelated in multiple ways.

As we reflect on our culture, readers should note that gaining a critical grasp on one's culture is no easy thing. Culture is like the water that a fish swims in. Margaret Silf tells the instructive story about a fish that heard that there was this thing called the sea. It decided to investigate, and swam and swam, searching in vain. The point is, of course, that it was so immersed in the sea that it couldn't even see it. We are too often just like that fish when it comes to our culture. Culture is profoundly formative, and we tend to assume that "this is just how things are." Often, it is only when we travel that we return with fresh eyes to our own culture to see it for the first time, warts and all.

How then should we characterize Western culture today?

First, we live in modernity, that epochal era that emerged out of the Enlightenment and post-Enlightenment eras in the West. The engine driving modernity was provided by philosophy and the scientific and historical revolutions. At the heart of modernity is a stress on human autonomy and the capacity for reason and science to facilitate unprecedented progress. Indeed, at the outset of the 20th century, there was a hubris abroad that, with our science and technology, we would solve all the world's problems and usher in a kind of utopia.

Modernity has, in fact, brought many good gifts. None of us would like to go back to an age before anesthesia! Healthy democracy is a good form of government, and the benefits of technology are apparent to all. However, technology is also a good example of a benefit with a shadow side. Without argument the Internet ushered in a revolution in accessibility to pornography from around the world; it's now available to anyone, anywhere with an Internet connection, unless strong efforts are made to filter it.

Modernity also has a centrally anti-Christian dimension. For progress to be made, it was believed, we needed to be free from the constraints of tradition and dogma. In the West, this has evolved into a doctrine of "freedom of religion," but in reality this is freedom of a *privatized* religion. From this perspective, we are free to believe as we wish provided we keep our beliefs out of the great public spheres of life, such as education, politics, health care, economics, and so on. In these spheres, neutral, autonomous reason must reign.

In the name of postmodernism, which began in the 1980s in the West, many of the ideological underpinnings of modernity have been severely mauled, coming as postmodernism did at the end of the most brutal century in history. In my view, postmodernism is not *post*modernity but is the unraveling of the DNA of modernity. In his *The Condition of Postmodernity*, geographer David Harvey analyses postmodernity in depth but also provides a handy way for grasping it.[45] Modernity rejected religion and tradition as the way to truth and sought through autonomous reason to arrive at the truth of our world. Postmodernism no longer believes that such truth is available but rejects a return to tradition and religion. The result is that we are left with nihilism. In previous decades nihilism would have been a cause for great concern, but postmoderns encourage us to celebrate it in a kind of cheerful nihilism.[46]

Postmodernism is insightful in challenging the neutrality of modernity. What was presented as neutral and autonomous has been shown again and again to be anything but. The Holocaust, for example, showed us just what could be "accomplished" with modern technology: two world wars; the emergence of Marxism and its embodiment, however incompletely, in the Eastern Bloc leading to genocidal purges; the environmental crisis; and so on. By the end of the 20th century it was impossible to confidently affirm the modern project, and this questioning is central to postmodernism. However, postmodernism, by its refusal to retrieve orthodox religion and tradition, has ended up with little positive to offer. Furthermore, postmodernism remained in the liberal Western tradition with its embrace of human autonomy. As Gadamer commented at the dialogue at Capri on religion, of course we cannot go behind Kant![47]

While philosophically modernity has been savaged by postmodernism, in other ways it continues to triumph. The technological revolution continues apace, and globalization has spread consumer capitalism to every corner of the world. Consumerism has become *the* ideology of our day, without many of the constraints that modern ideology previously exercised on it. To a significant extent, consumerism is driven by greed and the love of money, ideologies that are clearly unsustainable. French anthropologist René Girard has drawn our attention to the role of mimetic desire in human relationships and culture building: We naturally model ourselves on one another, but such mimesis can become rivalry, and when this escalates it bursts forth in violence. Global consumer culture has generated what geographer Harm De Blij calls an economic apartheid between North and South, a veritable cauldron of desire with frightening potential for violence.[48]

I am sure this sounds highly theoretical, and the reader may rightly wonder what this has to do with preaching. In fact, a great deal! In his *Seventeen Contradictions and the End of Capitalism*, David Harvey has an insightful

discussion of the house/home under his first contradic-
tion between use value and exchange value. Harvey rightly
notes that a house has many functions or uses: It provides
shelter; it is a place where couples build a home and an af-
fective life; it is "a site of daily and biological reproduction
(where we cook, make love, have arguments, and raise children)";[49] it provides for privacy and security in an unstable
world; and so on. Christians have a vested interest in the
well-being of the home, which some Catholics delightfully
describe as the "domestic church." We should therefore be
keenly alert to Harvey's point that in much of the more advanced capitalist world, "housing is built speculatively as a
commodity to be sold on the market to whoever can afford
it and whoever needs it."[50] He notes that the aim of those
building and providing housing is to secure exchange values and *not* use values. He asserts:

> Housing provision under capitalism has moved,
> we can conclude, from a situation in which
> pursuit of use values dominated to one where
> exchange values moved to the fore. In a weird
> reversal, the use value of housing increasingly
> became, first, a means of saving and, second,
> an instrument of speculation for consumers
> as well as producers, financiers and all the oth-
> ers (real estate brokers, loan officers, lawyers,
> insurance agents etc.) who stood to gain from
> boom conditions in housing markets. The pro-
> vision of adequate housing use values ... for the
> mass of the population has increasingly been
> held hostage to these ever-deepening exchange
> value considerations. The consequences for the
> provision of adequate and affordable housing
> for an increasing segment of the population
> have been disastrous.[51]

With the breakdown in family life in the West we will undoubtedly find ourselves preaching on family life, developing stable, creative homes, and so on. But it is imperative that when we do so we are aware that our middle-class congregation members will be caught between the tension of the home as a consumer product and the home *as a home*. Then one can begin to see the prophetic insight in Scott Russell Sanders' comment that "real estate ads offer houses for sale, not homes. A house is a garment, easily put off or on, casually bought or sold; a home is skin. Merely change houses and you will be disoriented; change homes and you bleed. When the shell you live in has taken on the savor of your love, when your dwelling has become a taproot, then your house is a home."[52] We should also be aware that our congregation may be entirely middle class—there may be no mixed-income housing in our area if poorer folk simply cannot afford to live nearby.

Many of us will thus recall the debate in missiological circles about Donald A. McGavran's church-growth school, with its emphasis on focusing on monochrome parts of the population. A legitimate critique of the church-growth school was that the glory of the New Testament church is its diversity, with rich and poor sitting alongside one another. The church was the one place in society where slave and master, poor and wealthy, came face to face as brothers and sisters in Christ. Those of us who minister in middle-class suburbs will know that, de facto, we are back in McGavran's situation. With the house as a commodity, prices continue to climb, and it may be that only a very select group of society can afford to live near our church. Similarly, poor areas will be monochrome in the reverse way. Thus, it becomes impossible to reproduce the diversity of the people of God that New Testament letters such as James portray, unless we become conscious of the depth and comprehensive repentance the gospel may call us to.

What does the preacher do, then, when explaining James to the congregation? We rarely reflect on just how deeply such letters challenge multiple dimensions of our lives, and we complete our series of sermons without having allowed Scripture to penetrate into the marrow and bone of our worlds. Were we to do so, all sorts of interesting questions would emerge: Are there different ways of doing housing? So we're in suburbia, but can we change it? And to our surprise we will discover that, yes, there are different ways of doing housing, ways that promote community and cater to wealthy and less wealthy. In his brilliant *Till We Have Built Jerusalem*, for example, Arthur Bess suggests that if a church has several acres on which to build a church that they do so, but also that they lay the foundations for a different style of community, with mixed-income housing and some shops for local produce, shops that would subvert the insane monochrome chains that are imposed on city after city by the corporate world.[53]

If modernity emerged out of the West, the centers of economic and political power are now changing. A few years ago I was fortunate enough to visit South Korea and learned to my astonishment just how advanced that country is in so many ways. I returned with a sense of the decline of the West and of a rapidly changing world. Western-style consumerism is clearly unsustainable, and in 2008 the bubble nearly burst. Our North American culture teaches us to see that as a blip so that if we just get out and spend more money, exponential growth will resume—a myth if ever there was one. The result is that in many ways, the West is in crisis both ideologically and economically.

Amid this crisis we are witnessing the emergence of virulent forms of secularism. The New Atheism is one such example. Ironically, at the same time globally we are in the midst of a major resurgence of religion, and especially of orthodox Christianity in the developing nations, as Philip Jenkins has repeatedly drawn to our attention. Living in the West we need to take seriously the title of his best-known book, *The Next Christendom*.[54] It is in developing countries that Christianity is growing fast, and we would do well to develop alliances and relationships with churches in these countries *now*—in a new world order we may need them far more than they will need us.

The secular West is being forced to reassess the role of religion not least through the challenge of radical Islam. Until the explosion of radical Islam in the West most political commentators simply did not have a lens through which to take religion seriously at the public level. Like Christianity, Islam is also growing fast in the developing world and in Africa, for example, we are close to a situation where one out of every two Africans is either Christian or Muslim. This means that one of the most serious issues facing nations today is that of *pluralism*. Years ago James Sire wrote his classic *The Universe Next Door*.[55] The title is evocative; we may well find ourselves living next door to people who conceive of the universe in a radically different way.

Intriguingly, this is also a time of great opportunity for Christianity in the West. Western democracies have, for example, found that their charity bills are getting bigger and bigger but without being effective in alleviating poverty. Prior to the Charitable Choice legislation in 1996 in the United States, religious organizations were not eligible for government funding for charitable work unless they divested themselves of all their religious particularity and essentially operated as secular organizations. The insight dawned that it is generally *religious* groups that live and work among those needing help, and Charitable Choice opened the door for religious organizations to apply for government funding for charitable activities without having to divest themselves of their particularities. Similar moves have taken place in the United Kingdom. Radical Islam potentially throws a wrench in such works, but the need for healthy religion that genuinely serves the poor and facilitates upliftment is all the more clear.

Such is the power of globalization that no country is untouched by it. I grew up in South Africa and return there each year. It is a beautiful country and one close to my heart. However, the challenges it faces are legion. Having emerged out of the dark days of apartheid, hopes ran high, but nowadays such hope is diminished by the challenges of crime, poor governance, corruption, and so on. Many who worked tirelessly against apartheid are raising the alarm about current trends, but what is surprising is that few commentators note that South Africa's challenges need to be diagnosed at the intersection of its own history and its encounter with globalization. The release of Nelson Mandela and the unbanning of the African National Congress and other organizations opened the world again to South Africa, for better and for worse. The first major corruption scandal that hit the new South Africa was an arms deal, the truth of which is still not known. Sadly, Western corporations played a key role in this corruption.

One cannot understand the challenges of South Africa without exploring the interface between its own story and its interaction with globalization. And so it will be with our particular cultures. Canada, for example, has a very different history from South Africa, but it too is at the interface between its own history and globalization. The preacher will need to be immersed in his or her own culture while deeply aware of global turns and how they impact us on a daily basis.

And then there is one's particular congregation. The local congregation is *the* place, the airport, where the plane of the sermon is to be landed week in and week out. In recent decades, missiology has recognized the vital importance of the local congregation. Lesslie Newbigin, for example, speaks of the hermeneutic of the local congregation, meaning that it is in and through the local congregation that the gospel is to be interpreted and made real and plausible in the world.[56] The captain of the plane is the Spirit, but, in cooperation with the Spirit, preachers need to become experts in landing the plane. The pastor/ preacher is set aside by the sheep, and generally paid by them, to keep *them* attentive to God.

One sometimes meets pastors who love preaching but dislike counseling and pastoral work. In some pastoral teams, duties are split along such lines. The danger of this should be obvious: How can one land the plane without knowing the congregation intimately, with all their joys, struggles, and challenges? Alas, research reveals that the gap between preaching and the existential needs of congregations is far too often real. H. J. C. Pieterse, in his fine book *Communicative Preaching*, reports, "Empirical research has revealed deficiencies in preaching practice as regards the congregation's actual reception of the message. The main problem is that preachers do not know precisely what their congregations' needs, ideas, and reflections are. Their world is too far removed from that of the congregation."[57]

In Revelation 1:13 Christ is described as "among the lampstands," the lampstands representing individual churches. If Christ walks in our midst, closely attentive to the health of his people as the "light of the world" (Matt 5:14), how much more so should this be true of the pastor and the flock? Preachers need to be pastors, and as such they need to be immersed in the lives of their congregations. A deep capacity for relationship and for confidentiality is essential. Coffee together after the Sunday service is important, but woefully insufficient if that is all the contact the preacher has with the people. Most of church members' lives are lived outside the institutional church, and the preacher needs to be meeting with them where they spend most of their lives—in the workplace, at home, on the sports field, and so on. A relational bridge needs to be constructed between the sheep and the shepherd so that there is constant traffic between the two. Only thus will the preacher gain that intimate knowledge of the congregation, for whom he or she tries week after week to land the plane of the sermon.

In my opinion we need to do hard and thorough work in this area. Relationship is indispensable, but empirical research can also be a great help. When I studied in the United Kingdom, I noticed that churches were audited to identify strengths and weaknesses. We have to have our finances audited, but for the rest, we stroll along, never thinking that there is so much at stake in the local church and in our preaching that it might warrant an audit.

There has been a growing recognition that biblical preaching is a two-way street—or, as practical theologians like to call it, "dialogical." The congregation, and not just the preacher, are responsible for receiving God's Word. Vicedom, for instance, recognizes the unique role of the apostles but goes so far as to say that Paul "does his work in the name of the church and the church is responsible along with him for his work. Both are implied in Paul— the apostolic authority and the co-responsibility of the church."[58] Elders and bishops, according to Vicedom, "are only watchmen whose concern it is that the building is really continued on the foundation of the apostles. They themselves are not the foundation."[59] The preacher is the instrument by which Christ addresses his people, but *their* reception and response to his word are equally important. As Vicedom asserts:

> Certainly the Lord present in His activity must be everything. But where the Lord is, there a visible congregation comes into being and lives not only in the proclamation, but *above all in the hearing*, which is the prerequisite for the witnessing. The church also lives in the love which through Christ becomes effective in her precisely *through the hearing*. She lives in adoration and doxology. She lives in the Sacrament and thereby in fellowship with her exalted Lord.[60]

We may think we have landed the plane on a particular Sunday, but how do we know whether this is actually the case? If hearing the Word is as important as proclaiming the Word, then we will need to attend closely and *creatively* to the reception of the Word by the congregation.

I do not for a moment want to detract from the importance of the preaching itself, but to enhance it. Along these lines, John Stott notes, "The average congregation can have a far greater influence than it realizes on the standard of preaching it receives, by asking for more biblical and contemporary sermons, by setting their pastors free from administration so that they may have more time to study and prepare, and by expressions of appreciation and encouragement when their pastors take their preaching responsibility seriously."[61] It needs to be said that preachers should take their task very seriously indeed. In my view the church is the primary place where God's Word is to be received, so that the brief message quickly prepared, and barely noticeable amid the rest of the service, is an aberration of the high calling of the preacher. I do not want to pontificate about sermon length; some preachers can preach long and you barely notice, while others are not gifted in this way. But whether short or long, one should be assured that hard work on the text and the sermon has gone into the preparation. There is much to be said about the state of biblical scholarship today, but enough good work is being done that Western preachers at least are without excuse when it comes to having a series of good commentaries available on whatever text they are preaching from. Where we have training in Greek or Hebrew, this needs to be kept alive as we dig deeply, week by week, to uncover the pearl of great price in the field of Scripture.

If I may speak personally for a moment as a biblical scholar, many of us—albeit a minority in the guild—have devoted our lives to doing work on the Bible that is of service to the church and have worked hard to try to redirect biblical scholarship in this direction. In my view, we biblical scholars are like those behind the scenes while preachers are at the front lines. Both roles are indispensable for the great work to which we are called, and we need a healthy partnership between the two. Nowadays, alas, it is unusual for scholars to take preaching seriously, and it is too often unusual for preachers to take scholarship seriously. The result is that both settle for mediocrity, whereas together we need to strive for excellence.

As Stott points out in the above quote, congregations have a vital role to play in encouraging excellence in preaching. The most important contribution they play is to receive the Word, and we need to create the space for this to come to the fore. For example, there is no reason why preaching should not be complemented with creating space and time for a congregation to discuss their reception of the Word and what it means for their lives. This could take many different forms. One might, for example, include in the service a time after the preaching for the congregation to break into small groups to discuss what God is saying to them and what this means for them. There could be brief reports back from the groups in the service. Another model is practiced by a pastor friend of mine in South Africa. The church's small groups explore the text for the coming Sunday in *the week before* the text is preached on, thus ensuring that the congregation has already spent time with the text in a small-group context.

In brief, we need to find multiple creative ways to engage the congregation as fully as possible in listening to the Word. If one is planning an expository series on a book of the Bible, we could encourage members to purchase an accessible commentary on that book and work through it as we together move through the book week by week. Certainly one should not end a series on a book without the congregation emerging far more at home in that book *as a whole* than they were before. Again, we need to find creative ways to test and explore just what kind of reception is actually taking place.

LANDING THE PLANE: SOME EXAMPLES

In this final section we will look at examples of what it might mean to land the plane when preaching on particular biblical texts.

Example 1: Galatians 1:10–2:21

A cursory reading of Galatians indicates that the churches of Galatia were in deep trouble. In this section of Galatians, Paul defends his being an apostle. He produces at least six lines of evidence, namely:

1. His reception of the gospel by special revelation
2. His reception of the gospel independent of the apostles in Jerusalem and the Judaean churches
3. His early activities as a Christian
4. His first visit to Jerusalem after becoming a Christian
5. His second visit to Jerusalem 14 years later
6. His rebuke of Peter at Antioch

The *telos* of this section is clear: It is a robust defense of the validity of Paul's apostleship. Now, according to some theorists of preaching, it is *this telos* or message that we are called to preach! If that were the case, then once we agreed on the *telos* of a text, all of our sermons on a given text would look remarkably similar. Undoubtedly, there will be always be value in reminding a congregation that the apostles are the foundation of the church, that their testimony is what we have in the New Testament, and that a criterion for the canonicity of the New Testament is apostolicity.

However, Paul is addressing a particular problem in the Galatian churches. If you are in a congregation that, like the Galatians, doubts Paul's authority as an apostle, then you may well need to preach the *telos* of the text, but many of us are not in such situations. How then does one preach a text like this in a context in which Paul's apostleship is *not* an issue? Remember that the sermon emerges at the interface of the trajectory of the *telos* of the text and the context of the congregation. Thus, the preacher will have to ask: How does *this* text speak authoritatively *today* to *this* congregation? The answer is that many different, but quite legitimate, sermons can and will be preached from this text—but let me make a few suggestions as to how one might proceed.

Paul is responding to a problem that the Galatians had with *authority*, and his authority as an apostle in particular. One could therefore ask: In modernity and in our congregation, do we have any comparable trouble with authority, and in particular the authority of God addressed to us through his Word?

The minute one asks this question about modernity, one starts to realize what explosive material one is dealing with in Galatians. To a significant extent, modernity is premised on the rejection of religious authority and the assertion of human autonomy. Special revelation is regarded as suspect and certainly of no public significance. Indeed, Jewish sociologist Philip Rieff argues that culture making always involves the translation of sacred order into social order but that for the first time in history we in the West live in a context in which we are trying to do without sacred order.[62] In a nutshell, we are trying to do life, in all its dimensions, without God. As Rieff points out, this is catastrophic, and the consequences will be legion.

Modernity is our cultural context. Culture, as we explored above, is like the water a fish swims in, so it is exceedingly hard to get a critical grip on one's own culture. Unless we are alerted otherwise, we tend to regard our modern way of life as normal. Think of our example above about the house/home today. What could be more normal than a middle-class suburban town in which house prices keep escalating? I suggest it is profoundly abnormal from a biblical perspective. Unless we start landing the plane, our brothers and sisters will keep coming to church—we hope—while living lives that conform to modernity without a thought. Parents will send their children to be "discipled" at the best modern universities without a moment's thought about the ideologies governing their education, and then we will wonder why so many young adults lose their faith. Our businesspeople will operate according to corporate strategies without ever thinking these through carefully from a biblical perspective.

My hunch is, therefore, that in both preacher and congregation we will find far more of human autonomy at work than any of us might have suspected, and this passage in Galatians speaks profoundly to that issue, to any refusal to submit to the authority of the gospel, to the authority of God in all areas of life.

If you think this all sounds a bit deep, I offer no apology. If we think of the church as also sent and thus sharing in the "apostolate" with the apostles, Hoekendijk's words are salutary:

> The arena of the apostolate is the world. The content of the apostolate is the lifting up of the banners of salvation, of shalom; the apostolate becomes a reality in the kerygma, the public proclamation of shalom, in the koinonia, the corporative participation in shalom, and in the diakonia, the ministering demonstration of shalom.[63]

If the arena into which we are sent is the world, and if we wish to raise "the banners of shalom," then we had better know how the Word relates to and provides a lens for understanding our world. Years ago Franky Schaeffer, the son of Francis Schaeffer, wrote a book titled *Addicted to Mediocrity*.[64] One might well write a book on preaching today entitled *Addicted to Superficiality*, at least when it comes to landing the plane. Preachers are not called to be experts in all areas of life, but they will need to work hard on understanding both Word *and* world if they are to avoid superficial applications. Here again, is an area where preachers and Christian scholars ought to cooperate—that is, in the area of cultural analysis.

At the same time it is important to note how such an approach also lends itself to contextual evangelism. According to Genesis 3, at the very heart of sin is the rebellious quest for human autonomy, to be a law unto oneself. Vicedom rightly says:

> Through the exaltation Jesus becomes Lord over all hostile powers seeking to destroy God's work of salvation, and He becomes Lord also over that other world which comprises the kingdom of darkness. He becomes the Head of His church. Thus God solves all the great central questions which have ever agitated religious people, not as man imagined, but in His own way, and therefore in an absolutely valid manner. *Man is lifted out of his self-deification and again made into a creature and the vis-à-vis of God.* With Jesus Christ the time of darkness and ignorance ends.[65]

Humankind's self-deification is central to Western thought and life today, as the debates about abortion, sexuality, health care, economics, education, other religions, and so on regularly reveal. At the heart of self-deification is the question of authority: Am I my own authority, or do I only truly find myself when I submit to this God who has come to me in Jesus Christ? As Vicedom says, "The wonderful thing about the Gospel is that under the Word of God man may become fully that which he is by birth."[66]

Example 2: Genesis 1:16

Scripture is diverse in its genres, and some parts speak far more directly to us than others. Richard Bauckham edited a book that argues that the Gospels were deliberately written for all Christians, and thus they are not overly directed at a particular group in the first century AD.[67] However, it is surprising just how much of Scripture is already contextualized. Take Genesis 1:1–2:3, for example. For years I doubted I could preach this text because I had been introduced to it through a very literal reading and in relation to modern questions about science, evolution, 24-hour days, and so on. A major insight for me was the realization that when Genesis 1 was written there were many stories of creation circulating in the ancient Near East at that time, and that the author of Genesis alludes to these and alerts his audience to how an Israelite approach to creation differs from a pagan one. To give one example: Both sun and moon were commonly worshiped as gods in the ancient Near East. If you read Genesis 1, you will note that the author never uses the Hebrew words "sun" and "moon" but refers to "the greater light" and "the lesser light" (Gen 1:16). Why? Deliberately to make the point that the sun and moon are part of God's creation and *not* gods. In other words, Genesis 1 says a firm "No!" to a pagan worldview that deifies some part of God's good creation and worships it as divine.

Doubtless there are people nowadays who worship the sun and the moon as gods, and to them one could preach the *telos* of Genesis 1:16 directly. In our Western context, however, few would even dream of such a thing. But paganism is alive and well in Western culture, since in terms of how humanity is made we cannot survive without treating something as divine. You can tell a person's god by looking closely at the thing from which they derive ultimate meaning. It could be logic and rationality—that is, "science"—or family life, or wealth, or personal achievement. Such is the fallenness of humans: that they will take anything as god rather than submit to the true God. The important point is that our paganism is very different from that addressed by Genesis 1:16; we will need to work hard to understand Genesis 1 and to see how this powerful text interfaces with current temptations toward paganism at work in our congregations and societies. Genesis 1:16 lends itself to powerful, contemporary evangelistic preaching, but believers, too, are vulnerable to paganism. In my reading of Job, his obsessive religiosity around his children in Job 1 hints at a problem: His religion was in danger of becoming a crutch to protect what was most important to him, namely his family.[68] Again and again, we try to replace God by absolutizing some part of his creation.

Example 3: Exodus 20:3

I suspect that many readers have preached a series on the Ten Commandments. To a significant extent they speak directly to us and at one level need little mediation via the approach recommended in this book. They are presupposed and affirmed in the New Testament, although the Sabbath command's applicability is debated. But even here a thoughtful approach can deepen our interpretation and preaching of the Ten Commandments.[69]

Reading the Bible as a grand story is illuminating in this respect. The Ten Commandments occur in act 3 of the drama of Scripture and so apply first to Israel as an ancient Near Eastern nation in covenant with Yahweh. Indeed, they are at the heart of the Sinai covenant, spelling out what is utterly central if the Israelites are to be Yahweh's people and he to be their God.

What might one call a series on the Ten Commandments? I can think of few better titles than Patrick Miller's description of the commandments as "the ethos of the good neighborhood."[70] Israel's God is the creator God, and thus his law or instruction fits with the grain of creation so that the Ten Commandments are the signposts toward human flourishing, toward life as God intends it to be! They are not bad news but good news—gospel.

However, they are given to the nation Israel, and in act 5 of the drama of Scripture God's people are no longer a nation but spread throughout the nations of the earth. They are also given to the *ancient Near Eastern* nation of Israel and reflect this historical and cultural particularity. Take the first commandment, for example. I agree with the view, as noted above, that what it forbids is the worship of any other gods in the sanctuary and temple of Israel. This, I take it, is the meaning of "before me." In the ancient Near East it was common practice to have multiple gods in the system; in many ways, the more the merrier! Not so in Israel. Not only was there no representation of Yahweh—a scandal in the ancient Near East—but no other gods were to be represented.[71] In practice, Israel was monotheistic, even if the full implications of this dawned more slowly.

Thus, the first commandment speaks about purity of worship and rejects idolatry, a perennial temptation of the Israelites. It evokes Yahweh's jealousy and refusal to allow rivals among his people.

Act 4 of the drama of Scripture changes the structures and institutions of God's people in radical ways. No longer is there a central sanctuary; now, God's people worship in spirit and truth in millions of places throughout the world. Furthermore, in the West today we are unlikely to set up a shrine with multiple gods represented. Times have changed, but the challenge of pure worship and rejection of idolatry remains. In all my years of listening to sermons I cannot recall hearing one on purity of worship. However,

the first commandment is clear that worship can be con-
taminated. How might that be the case today? This is the
crucial question if we are to land the plane. And what are
the peculiar dangers in our congregation in this respect?

An example of contamination is the sort of liberal
preaching we referred to in the introduction, where the
sermon is aimed right into our contemporary world in the
name of the Lord, but one has no idea where it has come
from. Evangelicals also are not immune to using Scripture
to tell the congregation what they want them to hear rather than what the Word is saying.

Let me focus rather on the "no to idolatry" of the first
commandment. Idolatry emerges whenever humans as-
cribe ultimate worth to something other than the living
God. How, I ask you, can one land this plane, full of dyna-
mite as it is, without some sense of the idols of our day and
their possible manifestation in our congregation? Without
an informed sense of the idols of our day, we will reduce
this commandment to trivialities. Dutch economist Bob
Goudzwaard, my good friend, wrote a book titled, in its
English translation, *Idols of Our Time*, and it is this sort of
analysis we will need if we are to land the plane of this
text.[72] Only thus will there be any hope of this text doing
its searing work amid our people, weaning us off the idols
with which modernity is awash so that we might truly live
today as the people of God.

In apartheid South Africa, where I grew up, we were
awash in the idolatry of racial purity and the superiority
of whites and European culture. The entire world could
see this, but most South African evangelicals could not
or chose not to. There is a lesson to be learned from this:
Culture is so much a part of us that it is hard to see what
is shaping and forming us from day to day. The South, for
example, can see that the North is awash in consumer

capitalism, but we in the North think that we have a right to *more*. Canadian Catholic philosopher Charles Taylor wrote an important little book titled *The Malaise of Modernity*, and this might be the sort of place to start, alongside Goudzwaard's *Idols of Our Time*, to get a grip on the water in which we swim and preach.[73]

Example 4: Ephesians 6:10–20

Spiritual warfare is a hot topic nowadays, and many of the readers of this book will have preached a series on the armor of God. This section must be read both within Ephesians as a whole and within the context of the canon of Scripture. A common designation for God in the Old Testament is Yahweh of Hosts, and many think that the "hosts" are the armies of heaven. Thus, when we think of Christians in military mode, there is a real sense in which they are imaging God. As is typical of Paul's letters, Ephesians divides into a more doctrinal section and a more ethical section, namely chapters 1–3 and chapters 4–6 (cf. Rom 1–11; 12–16). Having set out in a magisterial way the extent of what God has done in Christ and then explored the implications for the lives of his readers, Paul draws his letter to a conclusion with this section on spiritual warfare. Why?

If you have ever traveled on the London Underground, you will be familiar with the repetitive announcement when getting on and getting off trains, "Mind the gap!" I suggest that this is what Ephesians 6:10–20 is about— namely, the gap between knowing the truth and living it. It is one thing to understand and have a keen sense of how the gospel should be lived, and quite another to actually translate it into everyday life. Paul is acutely aware of the resistance we face as we try, day by day, to live the gospel.

Hence, this final section on spiritual warfare as the means to overcome the gap.

Ephesians is more like the Gospels than Paul's other letters in that it is most likely a general letter to a number of churches. We suspect this because some of the early copies of the Greek manuscripts of Ephesians do not include the words "in Ephesus" in Ephesians 1:1. Nevertheless, I hope to show how our approach to preaching remains illuminating even for a book that is less situationally specific than others. Indeed, a sense of the context in which we preach can illuminate not only application but also our reading of Ephesians 6.

I recall preaching a series on the armor of God in my early days as a minister. Every part of the armor was explored in detail, and I aimed at having everyone of my congregation fully equipped with each piece of the armor. Alas, I treated this passage in an entirely individualistic way, sending out each "soldier" to fight the battles of life by themselves. Western individualism is one of the "malaises of modernity" that Charles Taylor discusses, and I had simply read my own appropriation of individualism from my culture into the text. However, if you read this passage in the Greek, you will discover that the imperatives are all in the second-person *plural*! Paul's readers are called to put on the armor of God together and as a whole. No soldier in Paul's day would ever consider going into battle alone—this would be madness—but here I was sending my brothers and sisters off into battle alone. And, of course, the battle is far too dangerous and serious to be fought alone.

In terms of landing the plane, how might an awareness of our context help in preaching this text? Against Western individualism, we would need to preach the text communally, pointing out just how much we need each other if we are to fight with any hope of success. We know from Acts the sorts of battles Paul and the other apostles encountered in their day, but what are the battlegrounds of our day? Once again, Christian cultural analysis is indispensable. If we do not think this through carefully, we will end up trivializing spiritual warfare and locating the great battles of our day in Ninja Turtles and Harry Potter, as some have done! Martin Luther insightfully commented that if we fight everywhere except where the battle is raging, we do not fight at all.[74] Real, in-depth discernment is required if we are to help our congregations to identify the battles of our day and to help them to see how they are already immersed in these battles. Bear in mind that there are no shortage of voices in the media clamoring to tell us what we should see as the major issues of our day, issues such as the social justice of same-sex marriage, the threat to our biosphere, the individual right to assisted suicide, and so on. None of these is a simple issue, and we will need to think through them carefully and with nuance. Indeed, it would be fascinating *before* preaching such a series to do a questionnaire with our congregation to see what they think are the major sites of spiritual warfare today. Such a questionnaire could be repeated after the series to see how perspectives have—or have not—changed.

I love the title of a book by Dutch philosopher Herman Dooyeweerd, *Roots of Western Culture: Pagan, Secular and Christian Options*. It evokes the breadth of the kingdom of God and the kingdom of darkness. The whole of creation belongs to God, and every sphere is contested by evil. We will need to work out where the battle is raging in our time and in our context. As a teenager in apartheid South Africa, I was converted to Christ, into vital, living evangelical Christianity. We were passionate about our faith, deeply evangelistic, but in all my years of being a member of a church and then a minister I cannot once remember hearing a searching call for repentance from racism. And yet the most oppressive racism was staring us in the face every day! Romans 13 would be preached in a conservative way with no call for repentance from racism. Of course such a call would have moved us toward politics, a no-go zone for most South African evangelicals. But we cannot choose where the battlegrounds are, and politics is often one of the most contested domains in God's creation. If that is where the battle is, then that is where it needs to be addressed. How the institutional church addresses such an issue is pertinent, but that it must be addressed is not.

In our changing geopolitical context, huge issues are at stake, and while personal spiritual warfare must never be ignored, neither must the great challenges of our day as they impinge on our lives and those of millions of others.

CONCLUSION

Landing the plane. I hope that by this stage we have a sense of the magnitude of what is at stake in preaching: nothing less than God's glory and the well-being of his people and his world. The Word is the field in which is hid the pearl of great price, and preachers are responsible for digging in that field so that Christ is held up to us again and again in all his majesty, glory, compassion, and relevance.

So where to from here? In conclusion, let me suggest some practical ways forward.

First, it is wise to begin with repentance. Preachers too easily become familiar with the holy act of preaching, and we need to repent and commit ourselves to preaching the Bible for all it is—and we are—worth. We need to recommit ourselves to the joint ministries of prayer and the

Word. For those of us in the academy, we need to repent of not taking preaching seriously, and especially if we are biblical scholars or theologians we need to commit ourselves to doing the very best work in service of the church.

Second, we need to prioritize preaching in our pastoral ministries. It will never be the only thing we do, but space must be carved out to prioritize it. We need to vow to avoid mediocrity and to commit ourselves to using all tools at our disposal to work hard and prayerfully at the text week in and week out, in good times and bad. Among other things, this will mean staying aware of the best biblical and theological work being done by scholars. In recent decades rich work has been done, for example, on the Psalter as a literary whole and on Proverbs as a literary whole.[75] This is work that can transform our preaching, and we need to be in touch with it.

Third, we need to get all the help we can in understanding our world and our particular congregation so we can repeatedly land the plane in our particular context. Where we have access to Christian (and non-Christian) scholars in disciplines like sociology, cultural studies, media, and so on, we ought to shamelessly cultivate such relationships.

Fourth, we need to alert our congregations repeatedly that reception of the Word is a communal task; we must ensure that church education programs are in place to improve biblical literacy. Yearly evaluations often deal with the business side of the institutional church, but we must devote time to what is at the heart of the life of the church: prayer, the Word, and discipleship and mission.

Fifth, as with spiritual warfare, we need to be aware that this task is bigger than any one of us. We need to join forces with fellow ministers, to nurture relationships with Christian academics, and to draw on the resources within our own congregations and denominations. Just as

Dietrich Bonhoeffer wrote a famous book called *The Cost of Discipleship*, my fellow preachers should be aware that what is advocated in this book—excellent preaching—will also involve *costly* preaching. In apartheid South Africa, preaching against racism could put one's life in danger. Biblical preaching *will* nurture God's people, but it will also meet with resistance, especially as we bring the idols of our day into focus.

Sixth and ultimately, the work of preaching is the work of the Spirit, a work he delights to engage in. Thus, all our work of preaching must be immersed in prayer and with a profound sense of dependence on the Spirit. Our work must be done in the spirit of the prayer that John Stott used for years before preaching:

> Heavenly Father, we bow in your presence.
> May your Word be our rule,
>   your Spirit our teacher,
> and your greater glory our supreme concern,
> Through Jesus Christ our Lord.
> Amen.[76]

APPENDIX A:
SUGGESTED READING

The footnotes in the text provide many resources for the reader to pursue.

For an introduction to biblical hermeneutics, including preaching, see Craig Bartholomew, *Introducing Biblical Hermeneutics: A Comprehensive Framework for Hearing God in Scripture* (Grand Rapids: Baker Academic, 2015).

On Christian spirituality, Eugene Peterson's many books are indispensable reading.

On mission and Western culture, I heartily recommend everything Lesslie Newbigin has written.

On missional church, see Michael W. Goheen, *A Light to the Nations. The Missional Church and the Biblical Story* (Grand Rapids: Baker Academic, 2011).

On Christianity and culture, see Bruce R. Ashford, *Every Square Inch: An Introduction to Cultural Engagement for Christians* (Bellingham, WA: Lexham Press, 2015).

Faithlife.com continues to provide an array of resources for pastors, including Logos Bible Software. Do also look out for emerging volumes in the Transformative Word series, edited by Craig Bartholomew.

APPENDIX B:
AN EXPANDED APOSTLES' CREED

Readers should note that the Apostles' Creed is reproduced in bold, unchanged apart from changing "Christ" to "Messiah."

I believe in God, the Father almighty,
    creator of heaven and earth,   ACT 1
        who created the world very good,
        and placed the first couple in Eden, a
        perfect home.
        There they succumbed to temptation and
        chose autonomy over obedience,
        with consequences for the entire creation,
        unleashing sin and destruction into God's
        good creation.   ACT 2
        God responded by choosing Abraham,
        through whom he vowed to recover his purposes for all nations.
        From Abraham's descendants God formed
        his people Israel,   ACT 3
        and placed them in the land of Canaan,
        to be a showcase to the world of life under
        God's reign.
        Israel's persistent disobedience led to the
        judgment of exile,
        announced by the prophets,
        who also proclaimed the coming day
        when God through his Messiah would establish his kingdom.

**I believe in Jesus the Messiah, his only
Son, our Lord,**   ACT 4
    **who was conceived by the Holy Spirit
and born of the virgin Mary.**
    He lived a full and perfect life,
    and in his public ministry he proclaimed
    and embodied the kingdom of God.
    **He suffered under Pontius Pilate,
was crucified, died, and was buried;
he descended to hell.
The third day he rose again
from the dead.
He ascended to heaven
and is seated at the right hand of God the
Father almighty.**
    From there he poured out the Spirit on the
    day of Pentecost,   ACT 5
    inaugurating the age of mission,
    in which the news and life of the kingdom
    are to be carried to all nations.
    **From there he will come to judge the liv-
ing and the dead**
    and inaugurate the new heavens and the
    new earth.   ACT 6
I believe in the Holy Spirit,
    **the holy catholic church,
the communion of saints,
the forgiveness of sins,
the resurrection of the body,
and the life everlasting. Amen.**

ENDNOTES

1. See Craig G. Bartholomew and Bob Goudzwaard, *The Archaeology of Modernity* (Downers Grove, IL: IVP Academic, forthcoming).

2. Walter E. Williams, "Mankind's Most Brutal Century—Why?," 1 January 2000, http://econfaculty.gmu.edu/wew/articles/99/brutal-century.htm.

3. Lesslie Newbigin, *Trinitarian Doctrine for Today's World* (Eugene, OR: Wipf and Stock, 1988), 17–18.

4. Ibid., 18.

5. On this issue, see John R. W. Stott, *I Believe in Preaching* (London: Hodder and Stoughton, 1982), 137–44.

6. Ibid., 140.

7. Ibid., 144.

8. Leon Morris, *The Gospel According to John*, 2nd ed., New International Commentary on the New Testament (Grand Rapids: Eerdmans, 1995).

9. Karl Barth, *Chuch Dogmatics* vol. 3, *The Doctrine of Creation*, part 1 (Edinburgh: T&T Clark, 1986), 282.

10. See Gordon J. Wenham, "Sanctuary Symbolism in the Garden of Eden Story," *Proceedings of the 9th World Congress of Jewish Studies* 9 (1986): 19–25.

11. Craig G. Bartholomew, *Where Mortals Dwell: A Christian View of Place for Today* (Grand Rapids: Baker Academic, 2011), 26-27.

12. The NIV, like most translations, translates *logos* as "Word."

13. See the major commentaries on John.

14. Karl Barth, *Church Dogmatics*, vol. 1, *The Doctrine of the Word of God*, part 1 (Edinburgh: T&T Clark, 2004), 61.

15. Georg F. Vicedom, *The Mission of God: An Introduction to a Theology of Mission*, trans. Gilbert A. Thiele and Dennis Hilgendorf. (St. Louis: Concordia, 1965), 91.

16. Ibid., 92.

17. Eugene Peterson, *The Contemplative Pastor* (Grand Rapids: Eerdmans, 1993), 5: "How can I lead people into the quiet place beside the still waters if I am in perpetual motion?"

18. Ed Stetzer, "How Protestant Pastors Spend Their Time," *Christianity Today*, December 29, 2009, www.christianitytoday.com/edstetzer/2009/december/how-protestant-pastors-spend-their-time.html.

19. Eugene Peterson, *Working the Angles: The Shape of Pastoral Integrity* (Grand Rapids: Eerdmans, 1987), 1–2.

20. Eugene Peterson, *The Pastor: A Memoir* (New York: HarperOne, 2011).

21. Peterson, *Working the Angles*, 2.

22. Luke 9:33 NIV: "Master, it is good for us to be here. Let us put up three shelters—one for you, one for Moses, and one for Elijah."

23. William J. Dumbrell, *Covenant and Creation* (Exeter, UK: Paternoster, 1984).

24. This is the Goheen family version.

25. See Craig G. Bartholomew and Michael W. Goheen, *The Drama of Scripture: Finding Our Place in the Biblical Story*, 2nd ed. (Grand Rapids: Baker Academic, 2014), and Bartholomew and Goheen, *The True Story of the Whole World* (Grand Rapids: Faith Alive, 2009).

26. Lesslie Newbigin, *The Gospel in a Pluralist Society* (Grand Rapids: Eerdmans, 1989), 89.

27. Erich Auerbach, *Mimesis: The Representation of Reality in Western Literature* (Princeton, NJ: Princeton University Press, 2013).

28. Eugene Peterson, "Living into God's Story," originally posted on *TheOOZE: Conversation for the Journey*, http://www.biblicaltheology.ca/blue_files/Living%20into%20God's%20Story.pdf.

29. See Michael W. Goheen and Craig G. Bartholomew, *Living at the Crossroads: An Introduction to Christian Worldview* (Grand Rapids: Baker Academic, 2008).

30. See Craig G. Bartholomew, *Introducing Biblical Hermeneutics: A Comprehensive Framework for Hearing God in Scripture* (Grand Rapids: Baker Academic, 2015), for the relationship between narrative and drama in an analysis of the metanarrative of the Bible. For the Bible as a drama in five acts, see N. T. Wright, *The New Testament and the People of God* (Minneapolis: Fortress, 1992), 141–42; for six, see Bartholomew and Goheen, *Drama of*

Scripture. See also the excellent introduction to the Bible as a drama in six acts in the various versions of the Bible published by Biblica.

31. Wright, *New Testament and the People of God*, 140–43.

32. B. S. Childs, *Biblical Theology of the Old and New Testaments: Theological Reflections on the Christian Bible* (Minneapolis: Fortress, 1992), 725.

33. Gordon J. Spykman, *Reformational Theology: A New Paradigm for Doing Dogmatics* (Grand Rapids: Eerdmans, 1992).

34. Cf. Craig G. Bartholomew, "Covenant and Creation: Covenant Overload or Covenantal Deconstruction," *Calvin Theological Journal* 30, no. 1 (1995): 11–33.

35. See Albert Wolters, *The Song of the Valiant Woman: Studies in the Interpretation of Proverbs 31:10–31* (Carlisle, UK: Paternoster, 2001).

36. See Richard J. Bauckham, *The Theology of the Book of Revelation* (Cambridge: Cambridge University Press, 2003).

37. For reference, see Abraham Kuyper, in James D. Bratt, ed., *Abraham Kuyper: A Centennial Reader* (Grand Rapids: Eerdmans, 1998), 461.

38. Oliver O'Donovan, *Desire of the Nations: Rediscovering the Roots of Political Theology* (Cambridge: Cambridge University Press, 1999), 3.

39. James D. G. Dunn, *Romans 9–16*, Word Biblical Commentary 38B (Dallas: Word, 1988).

40. Peter Brown, *Through the Eye of a Needle: Wealth, the Fall of Rome, and the Making of Christianity in the West 350–550 A.D.* (Princeton, NJ: Princeton University Press, 2014).

41. Weigel makes this point in more than one place. Cf. George Weigel, *The End and the Beginning: Pope John Paul II—The Victory of Freedom, The Last Years, The Legacy* (New York: Image, 2010), 195.

42. Newbigin, *Trinitarian Doctrine*, 18–19.

43. David Bosch, *Believing in the Future: Towards a Missiology of Western Culture* (Pennsylvania, UK: Trinity Press, Gracewing, 1995), 48.

44. See Adam K. Webb, *A Path of Our Own: An Andean Village and Tomorrow's Economy of Values* (Wilmington, DE: ISI, 2009).

45. David Harvey, *The Condition of Postmodernity: An Enquiry into the Conditions of Cultural Change* (Oxford: Blackwell, 1991).

46. See Gertrude Himmelfarb, *On Looking into the Abyss: Untimely Thoughts on Culture and Society* (New York: Vintage, 1994).

47. Jacques Derrida and Gianni Vattimo, eds., *Religion* (Cambridge: Polity, 1998).

48. Harm De Blij, *The Power of Place: Geography, Destiny, and Globalization's Rough Landscape* (Oxford: Oxford University Press, 2009).

49. David Harvey, *Seventeen Contradictions and the End of Capitalism* (London: Profile Books, 2014), 15–16.

50. Ibid., 17.

51. Ibid., 22.

52. Scott Russell Sanders, *Earthworks: Selected Essays* (Bloomington: Indiana University Press, 2012), 110–11.

53. Arthur Bess, *Till We Have Built Jerusalem: Architecture, Urbanism, and the Sacred* (Wilmington, DE: ISI Books, 2006).

54. Philip Jenkins, *The Next Christendom: The Coming of Global Christianity*, 3rd ed. (Oxford: Oxford University Press, 2011). See also his *The New Faces of Christianity: Believing the Bible in the Global South* (Oxford: Oxford University Press, 2006); *God's Continent: Christianity, Islam, and Europe's Religious Crisis* (Oxford: Oxford University Press, 2007).

55. James Sire, *The Universe Next Door: A Basic Worldview Catalog*, 5th ed. (Downers Grove, IL: InterVarsity, 2009).

56. Lesslie Newbigin, *The Gospel in a Pluralist Society* (Grand Rapids: Eerdmans, 1989).

57. H. J. C. Pieterse, *Communicative Preaching* (Pretoria, South Africa: Unisa Press, 1987), 75.

58. Vicedom, *Mission of God*, 63.

59. Ibid., 64.

60. Ibid., 86, emphasis added.

61. Stott, *I Believe in Preaching*, 12.

62. For a good introduction to Rieff's fertile thought, see Antonius A. W. Zondervan, *Sociology and the Sacred: An Introduction to Philip Rieff's Theory of Culture* (Toronto: University of Toronto Press, 2005).

63. J. C. Hoekendijk, "Die Kirche in Missionsdenken," *Evangelische Missionszeitschrift* 17 (1952): 10.

64. Franky Schaeffer, *Addicted to Mediocrity: 20th Century Christians and the Arts* (Wheaton, IL: Crossway, 1981).

65. Vicedom, *Mission of God*, 53, emphasis added.

66. Ibid., 106.

67. Richard Bauckham, ed., *The Gospels for All Christians: Rethinking the Gospel Audiences* (Grand Rapids: Eerdmans, 1998).

68. Craig G. Bartholomew, *When You Want to Yell at God: The Book of Job*, Transformative Word (Bellingham, WA: Lexham Press, 2014).

69. For a sense of the political consequences that can flow from obeying the ninth commandment, "You shall not give false testimony against your neighbor," see the courageous story of Bill Browder's Russian lawyer Sergei in Bill Browder, *Red Notice: A True Story of High Finance, Murder, and One Man's Fight for Justice* (New York: Simon and Schuster, 2015). For a sense of the trouble that the seventh commandment, "You shall not commit adultery," can get one into, see Mark 6:14-29.

70. Patrick D. Miller, *The Way of the Lord: Essays in Old Testament Theology* (Grand Rapids: Eerdmans, 2007).

71. This is what scholars refer to as "monolatry."

72. Bob Goudzwaard, *Idols of Our Time* (Downers Grove, IL: InterVarsity, 1984).

73. Charles Taylor, *The Malaise of Modernity*, CBC Massey Lectures (Toronto: Anansi, 1991).

74. "If I profess, with the loudest voice and the clearest exposition, every portion of the truth of God except precisely that little point which the world and the devil are at that moment attacking, I am not confessing Christ, however boldly I may be professing him. Where the battle rages, there the loyalty of the soldier is proved, and to be steady on all the battlefield besides is mere flight and disgrace if he flinches at that point" (Martin Luther, in *D. Martin Luthers Werke. Briefwechsel* (Weimar, 1930-), 3:81.

75. On the Psalter, see Craig Bartholomew and Andrew West, eds., *Praying by the Book: Reading the Psalms* (Carlisle, UK: Paternoster, 2011). On Proverbs see Craig Bartholomew, *Reading Proverbs with Integrity*, Grove Biblical Series B22 (Cambridge: Grove, 2001).

76. Stott, *I Believe in Preaching*, 340.

ABOUT THE AUTHOR

Reverend Professor Craig Bartholomew is the H. Evan Runner Professor of Philosophy and professor of religion and theology at Redeemer University College, Ancaster, Canada. He is an ordained Anglican priest and the author of many books. He is the series editor for Lexham's Transformative Word series.